Chronicles of Old New York

James Roman

Museyon

New York

Library of Congress Cataloging-in-Publication Data

Names: Roman, James, 1952-
Title: Chronicles of old New York : exploring Manhattan's landmark
  neighborhoods / James Roman.
Description: Second edition. | New York : Museyon, 2016. | Includes index.
Identifiers: LCCN 2015047835 | ISBN 9781940842080 (paperback)
Subjects: LCSH: New York (N.Y.)--Guidebooks. | Manhattan (New York,
  N.Y.)--Guidebooks. | Neighborhoods--New York (State)--New
  York--Guidebooks. | Historic sites--New York (State)--New
  York--Guidebooks. | Walking--New York (State)--New York--Guidebooks. | New
  York (N.Y.)--History--Miscellanea. | New York
  (N.Y.)--Biography--Miscellanea. | BISAC: TRAVEL / United States /
  Northeast / Middle Atlantic (NJ, NY, PA). | HISTORY / United States /
  State & Local / Middle Atlantic (DC, DE, MD, NJ, NY, PA).
Classification: LCC F128.18 .R66 2016 | DDC 974.7/1--dc23
LC record available at http://lccn.loc.gov/2015047835

Published in the United States by:
Museyon Inc.
1177 Avenue of the Americas, 5th Floor
New York, NY 10036

Museyon is a registered trademark.
Visit us online at www.museyon.com

ISBN 978-1-940842-08-0

1561204

Printed in China

Cities aren't built from bricks and steel alone. It takes dreamers and schemers, visionaries and risk-takers. For four centuries these adventurous spirits have been drawn to New York City, each leaving a mark that can still be seen today. The history of Manhattan is written in its streets; here's where to find it.

—James Roman

For Ben Heilman

who taught me many chronicles of old New York

View of New York from Brooklyn Heights, 1849

CHRONICLES OF OLD NEW YORK

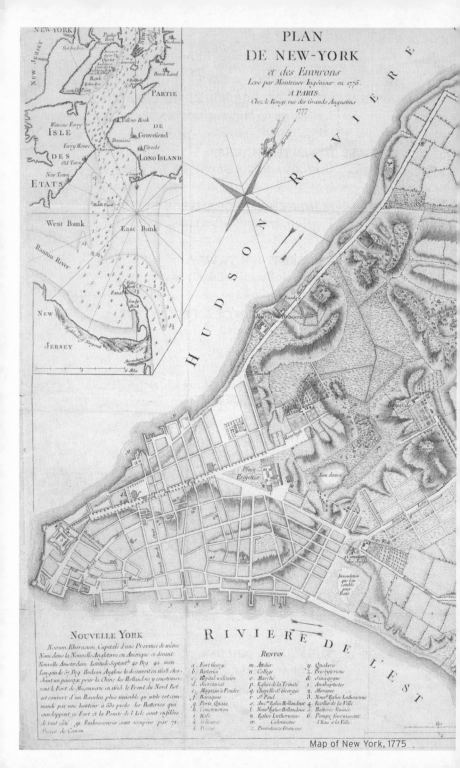

Map of New York, 1775

Key for Map
❶ Current location
⓪ Site no longer exists

CHAPTER 1

GEORGE WASHINGTON SLEPT HERE

WHEN NEW YORK WAS THE CAPITAL OF AMERICA

1789

America didn't gain its freedom from the British crown until October 19, 1781, when Lord Charles Cornwallis finally surrendered to George Washington's army after a five-day siege at Yorktown, Virginia. At that moment, almost all of New York City's landowners and merchants were British Loyalists patriotic to King George III. Roughly 15,000 of those Loyalists fled Manhattan, leaving their property behind, when American troops finally reoccupied the city on November 25, 1783. For decades, New Yorkers celebrated this date as Evacuation Day.

Of course, New York was a different place back then: The entire city consisted of a few hundred acres around Wall Street. Brooklyn was a far-off county, and properties as near as Gramercy Park were considered country estates.

City Streets

Pearl Street, originally known as Mother-of-Pearl Street due to all

View of Federal Hall of New York with the adjacent buildings in 1797

the iridescent shells embedded in its soil, follows an irregular path today because it once wound its way around the foot of a large hill. As Manhattan's population grew during the 1700s, new land was retrieved from the East River by leveling those hills, literally creating a street from the water: Water Street. By the mid-1780s, enough land had been moved in front of Water Street to pave yet another road along the waterfront, called Front Street.

The powerful DeLancey family controlled a massive parcel of that land, and maintained their loyalties to the king; James DeLancey was appointed New York's Chief Justice, to the displeasure of many New York colonists, while his father Etienne DeLancey, an enormously successful merchant, maintained the spacious family residence on Pearl Street at Broad Street. Before the defeat of Yorktown, the U.S. Congress declared all properties held by the British crown and its Loyalists to be forfeited. When Cornwallis surrendered, those lands were confiscated and sold. The obstinate DeLanceys, who had relied on a British victory to save their real estate dynasty, fell from power dramatically, forfeiting all the land from the Bowery to the East River, from Houston Street down to

Division Street. Over a mile of waterfront property was sold to fifteen leading families (the Roosevelts, Livingstons, and Beekmans among them), while the remaining parcels—each the size of one block—were sold to another 175 purchasers. As the British were driven from New York, the city's streets were promptly renamed: Crown Street became Liberty Street, King Street became Pine Street, Queen Street became Cedar Street. All that remains of the DeLanceys' reigning clout is a street with their name on the Lower East Side that even the triumphant colonists were too sentimental to change.

Washington Sleeps in New York

Thanks to its central location, the DeLanceys' home was converted into the Queen's Head Tavern in 1763, later renamed Fraunces Tavern for its proprietor Samuel Fraunces. (Restored by the Sons of the Revolution, it now stands as a public landmark at 54 Pearl Street.) It was here that General George Washington chose to bid farewell to his troops on December 4, 1783, before returning to Mount Vernon, his family home on the Potomac.

However, in 1785, the U.S. Congress moved to New York. City Hall, as the classically designed building on the corner of Wall Street at Broad Street was then known, became Federal Hall, serving as the first home of the U.S. Congress following the ratification of the Constitution. It was on the balcony of the original Federal Hall, overlooking Wall Street, that the first President of the United States delivered the first Inauguration Address on April 30, 1789, an emotional event marked by thunderous ovations from an enormous crowd.

George Washington's first Presidential Mansion, known as The Palace, at 3 Cherry Street

With New York then the nation's capital,

The Republican Court (Lady Washington's Reception Day) at the McComb house, Daniel Huntington, 1861

George Washington became one of Manhattan's most celebrated residents. But the leader of the nation's new government needed a home in the capital city. Samuel Osgood, whom Washington appointed to be the first Postmaster General, rented out his house at 3 Cherry Street to be the first Presidential Mansion, for 900 pounds a year. It was instantly known as The Palace, although the building was only three stories high. Not far from today's City Hall, the building was demolished to become the western foundation of the Brooklyn Bridge.

Its use as the Presidential Mansion was problematic, for Washington's stature was quite literal. Standing well over six feet tall, he was among the tallest men in America. The modest construction on the East River had ceilings that were too low, and it was, in the opinion of many New Yorkers, a location too far "out of town" to befit America's first president. So Washington moved. The second Executive Mansion was the McComb house at 39 Broadway, close to Federal Hall, a more fashionable Manhattan address. One year later, the U.S. Congress relocated to Philadelphia and George Washington left New York, never to return.

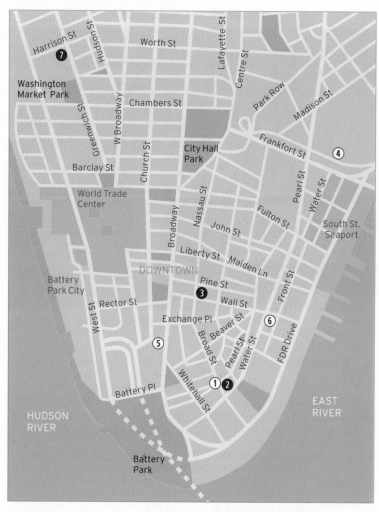

① DeLancey family home
   Pearl St. at Broad St.

❷ Fraunces Tavern
   54 Pearl St.

❸ Federal Hall
   Wall St. at Broad St.

④ Presidential Mansion
   3 Cherry St.

⑤ Second Presidential Mansion
   39 Broadway

⑥ Merchants' Coffee House
   Wall St. at Water St.

❼ Eighteenth-century houses
   Harrison St. at Greenwich St.

Taverns and Townhouses

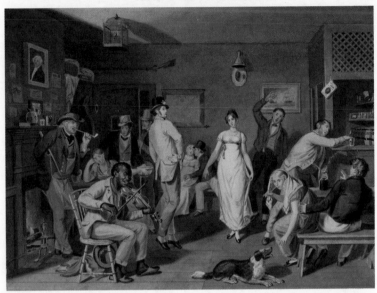

Taverns were the main place for socializing, posting notices and sharing news in early New York

Mass confusion defined New York City in the aftermath of the Revolutionary War. Loyalists raced out, soldiers returned home, and shrewd Americans seized confiscated properties at bargain prices. Locating friends and relatives was a daunting task. Churches and taverns were the main places to share news and post notices, and the most likely places to locate acquaintances.

At the Merchants' Coffee House (Wall Street at Water Street), where dice and backgammon were played amidst the celebrations of General Washington's victorious troops, a radical idea was hatched: a registry. All New Yorkers were encouraged to list their names and addresses,

permanent or temporary, which allowed returning friends and relatives to find them. Everyone in New York, it seems, made their way to the Merchants' Coffee House to participate in the inaugural registration process. After assembling data for three years, the city's first directory was published in 1786. (A year earlier, Philadelphia published a similar directory—the first in the New World.)

According to the first directory, nearly every block had a tavern. Of the 3,340 buildings in New York City, 330 held licenses permitting the sale of liquor. A tavern license cost 30 shillings (New York's currency was measured by pounds and shillings well into the nineteenth century), from which the Mayor and City Clerk each kept six shillings; the rest went to the city's treasury.

Very few original residential buildings still stand. Instantly recognizable by their pointed roofs, a row of early houses from 1796 was moved and restored on Harrison Street at Greenwich Street, where they exist now as privately owned residences with modern interiors. The exteriors of these landmark townhouses, however, are cherished examples of New York's earliest residential architecture.

CHAPTER 2

DRUNK ON WATER
AARON BURR'S PROFITABLE GAMBLE
1799–1842

"Don't drink the water!" had to be one of the perpetual cries from the Dutch settlers who founded New Amsterdam. In fact, those Dutch settlers were so parched during their first summer that they almost gave up and moved away. Things didn't improve quickly: For nearly 200 years, New York's water was so putrid even horses wouldn't drink it, and drunkenness couldn't be reprimanded since so many people had to mix spirits with their water just to swallow it.

Meanwhile, the solid bedrock that provides remarkable support for today's skyscrapers made drilling practically impossible for seventeenth-century settlers with primitive tools. The water they tapped underground was usually rainwater that seeped through the soil, contaminated along the way by all manners of impurities, and collected in depressions above the granite hulk that defines the island of Manhattan. One of the preferred pumps for drinking water was located just outside the walls of Trinity Church, where rainwater

Top: The Tea-Water Pump Garden provided drinkable water from a spring on what is now Park Row; bottom: The Croton Reservoir

was distributed after passing through hundreds of decomposing corpses in Trinity's graveyard.

The only decent, potable water came from a spring on what is now Park Row, between Baxter and Mulberry streets. A pump was placed over this spring and water for tea was sold to those who could afford it. Ornamental grounds were laid out around the pump, which became known as the Tea-Water Pump Garden, one of Manhattan's first parks. The well was four feet in diameter and twenty feet deep. The Tea-Water Pump was operated by an enormous handle that only the burliest men could manipulate. Its water cost three pence for 130 gallons at the pump, or one cent per gallon delivered to your door. "Tea Water Men" drove around Manhattan, selling water from heavy casks.

Corruption was inevitable. Tea Water was the only drinkable water in town, but was controlled by a group of thugs who made outrageous profits and whose wagons, waiting their turn to pass under the pump, blocked traffic for a mile in all directions. Something had to be done about the water situation.

In the fifteen years following the Revolutionary War, many individuals approached the Common Council with proposals to improve the water supply, but not until 2,000 New Yorkers died in an outbreak of yellow fever did the Council finally take action. They

The Tea-Water Pump at Roosevelt and Chatham Streets, Park Row

Aaron Burr, 1802

approved an idea presented by the unscrupulous politician Aaron Burr. He proposed the installation of wooden pipes leading from the pond adjacent to the Tea-Water Pump, which would provide running water to subscribers for $20 per year, an astronomical sum at the time.

Burr then maneuvered a bill through the State Legislature that granted a charter to The Manhattan Company, his private waterworks. It also included a cunning provision: The water company could use its "surplus capital in any manner not inconsistent with the constitution and laws of this State." On April 11, 1799, with Aaron Burr as Chairman of the Board, The Manhattan Company entered the waterworks business. A mere four months later, The Manhattan Company took their "surplus capital" and opened a bank. With capital stock of $2 million, the bank began operations at 40 Wall Street. Years later, The Manhattan Company became Chase Manhattan (currently JPMorgan Chase), the second largest retail bank in America during the twenty-first century.

Like a growing organism, New York City pushed its roots down into the earth: Thousands of logs were bored, laborers dug up the streets of Lower Manhattan, and new wooden pipes were buried five feet underground, two feet from the curb. With the main artery running down Broadway, The Manhattan Company laid six miles of wooden plumbing in its first year, providing water to 400 families. While the bank prospered, the waterworks were a constant nuisance.

Without meters, subscribers could run the water all they wanted. Non-subscribing friends were invited to take their fill from those who felt they paid too dearly for the poor-tasting water. Merchants gave it away for free to their steady customers. The wooden pipes proved to be impractical, as they were constantly lodged with debris. Subscribers often went for weeks without water, while The Manhattan Company tore up the streets to locate a clogged pipe and clear it, causing endless traffic jams. (Yes, Manhattan even had traffic jams in 1800.)

The Manhattan Company eventually laid twenty-five miles of wooden pipes, supplying water to 2,000 families, far short of its original plan. Although they tried, the company couldn't sell or lease its water rights without also losing its banking privileges. For forty more years, The Manhattan Company half-heartedly provided water to New Yorkers, while its bank flourished. Most New Yorkers chose to collect rainwater in backyard cisterns for free.

In 1832, contaminated water spread cholera, killing 3,500 New Yorkers. Finally admitting that Manhattan's wells and ponds were hopelessly polluted, the Common Council asked the voters to approve a dam on the Croton River in Westchester County, which would provide fresh water via an aqueduct into Manhattan. When the vote won on April 16, 1835, The Manhattan Company was off the hook, able to concentrate exclusively on banking.

New Yorkers ratified a closed-masonry aqueduct spanning forty-five miles. It led into a fifteen-million-gallon receiving reservoir at 86th Street (now Central Park), which in turn filled the distributing reservoir at Fifth Avenue and 42nd Street (where the New York Public Library is located today). The project cost $12 million and required six years of labor and 165 miles of plumbing to be laid under the streets of Manhattan. At dawn on June 22, 1842, the valve was opened and Croton River water began to fill the aqueduct. In Manhattan, people waited all day, having no idea of how long it would take for the water to reach them. Twenty-two hours later, at three o'clock the next morning, a cheer arose that lasted until the rushing water drowned it out.

On July 4, 1842, the Croton Distributing Reservoir at 42nd Street officially opened its tanks. Water gushed into the Reservoir while New Yorkers celebrated their fabulous new amenity. The

Croton Water Celebration, 1842

celebrations culminated when the aqueduct finally opened on October 14: church bells rang all day, 100 cannon blasts signaled the beginning of a five-mile parade and water spouted from fountains, hydrants and hoses. Firemen marched in the streets to the cheers of neighbors; President John Tyler also attended the festivities, along with former Presidents Martin Van Buren and John Quincy Adams. A fountain in City Hall Park gushed fifty feet high. Not only did New York finally have all the water it needed, it even had enough to waste.

New York was changed forever as crystal clear water roared through the conduits. New Yorkers were soon using thirty million gallons a day.

Townhouse construction blossomed as residents gave up their Greenwich Village cisterns for new homes with running water in developing neighborhoods such as Murray Hill, Turtle Bay, and Gramercy Park. Some folks landed on the east side, some headed west. For over a century, those neighborhoods developed the profiles that their proud residents cherish today. You know, it's in the water.

● Trinity Church
74 Trinity Pl.

② Tea-Water Pump Garden: Park Row
between Baxter and Mulberry sts.

③ Manhattan Company Building
40 Wall St.

❹ Receiving Reservoir
86th St. in Central Park

⑤ Distributing Reservoir
Fifth Ave. at 42nd St.

❻ City Hall Park

Key for Map

● Current location

⓪ Site no longer exists

CHAPTER 3

EARLY BOHEMIA
THE ROOTS OF GREENWICH VILLAGE

1822–1871

In 1789, when New York was America's capital, President George Washington lived in a house near today's Brooklyn Bridge, a short distance from Federal Hall, the hub of urban America. New York City was just a collection of narrow streets in today's Financial District. And where did Vice President John Adams live? In the suburbs! More precisely, John Adams lived in Greenwich Village.

Since the house stood on higher ground than the busy streets near Federal Hall, our fiery vice president, remembered as one of America's first activists, commuted on horseback to "the city" two miles away over gently rolling hills. As Adams' wife Abigail wrote: "In front of the house, the noble Hudson rolls his majestic waves." The Hudson River lapped up on a narrow sandy beach called Hudson Street, where the Adams children swam and fished. Minetta Brook emptied into a swamp between Charlton and Houston streets. It was a pastoral scene of fields and woodlands—but not for long.

Because of its high ground, Greenwich Village was considered a healthful area for summer homes, away from the noise and filth around Wall Street. When cholera, smallpox, and yellow fever turned "all streets below City Hall" into an "infected district" in 1822, thousands of New Yorkers evacuated to Greenwich Village to avoid the plague. The Village limits soon expanded as hills were flattened to accommodate transit, creating new streets to the west, and filling in the marshes to the east.

Adams' mansion, known as Richmond Hill, later became the home of Senator Aaron Burr. The humiliation that followed the tragic duel in which Burr killed Alexander Hamilton was a profitable opportunity for John Jacob Astor, the early real estate investor. To appease Burr's creditors, Astor foreclosed on the famous mansion, moved it to a flatter area down the street, then turned it into a tavern and a resort, later a series of theaters. Pastoral Greenwich Village was beginning to get raucous.

On nearby 3rd and 4th streets, French immigrants opened the saloons of "Frenchtown." Meanwhile, black girls danced in next-to-

Richmond Hill, home of John Adams and, later, Aaron Burr

nothing at the Black and Tan Concert Hall on Bleecker Street and Scotch Ann's was a brothel where whores were young men with painted faces and women's names.

Walt Whitman at Pfaff's saloon

Cozy cafés tucked away on winding streets attracted scores of writers, poets, actors, and intellectuals, who called themselves "bohemians" as they sought to maintain the lifestyles they once enjoyed in Paris. Walt Whitman patronized Pfaff's, his favorite beer hall at Broadway and Bleecker Street, where enthusiasts clustered to hear him read and speak. Essayist Ralph Waldo Emerson, who advocated anti-slavery and Transcendentalism among other new ideas, sniffed that the boisterous environment was strictly for "noisy and rowdy firemen." (Firemen were low-paid workers who shoveled coal to keep furnaces ablaze, not New York's Bravest, who fight fires.) Nonetheless, it was soon fashionable for denizens of other neighborhoods to venture to Greenwich Village for an evening of observing the bohemians with their curious behavior and colorful dress.

With little effort, bohemians turned Greenwich Village into one of New York's most entertaining districts, reaping a fortune for Astor, who sold almost sixty-two acres of the old Adams land to speculative builders. Many of the Federal townhouses within today's Charlton-King-Vandam Historic District were built by speculators who acquired their land from the Astors.

With its innocence lost, Greenwich Village provided another kind of diversion: collective rage. In 1837, New York University erected a Gothic Revival building on the northeast corner of the parade grounds at Washington Square, constructed from stones cut by convicts at Sing Sing, the maximum-security prison located about thirty miles up the river in Ossining, New York. The indignant stonecutters of New York's Stonecutters Guild promptly organized

The fatal duel between Aaron Burr and Alexander Hamilton, 1804

New York's first mass labor demonstration in Washington Square, which continued for days. To complete its construction, NYU was forced to call in the 27th Regiment of the National Guard to clear the demonstrators from the site.

It became clear that a diverse crowd could be addressed when any cause was proclaimed loudly enough within Washington Square. To the east, the lofty eyes of academia (New York University, to this day, remains the largest private educational institution in the United States), while on the north side, protestors could shout to the wealthy inhabitants that occupied magnificent townhouses. To the south, the bawdy proletariat of Frenchtown was always reliable when it came to radical causes, and to the west, the densest population of laborers in America.

Washington Square, which became a park in 1871, was suddenly the epicenter of Greenwich Village, a focal point for America and an ideal gathering place for the exercise of free speech. For more than a century, Washington Square has vigorously hosted Civil War riots, women's suffrage demonstrations, labor union rallies, racial equality rallies, teachers strikes, anti-war protests, draft card burnings, flag burnings, bra burnings, love-ins, smoke-ins, and gay rights demonstrations—the list goes on.

Today, Greenwich Village is one of the largest historic districts in the nation: its architecture is protected by landmark status. Far from musty, the Village continues to identify with its radical, bohemian past; its freethinking ambience is kept alive by young and old, rich and poor, gay and straight residents all living together side-by-side.

Somewhere, John Adams is smiling.

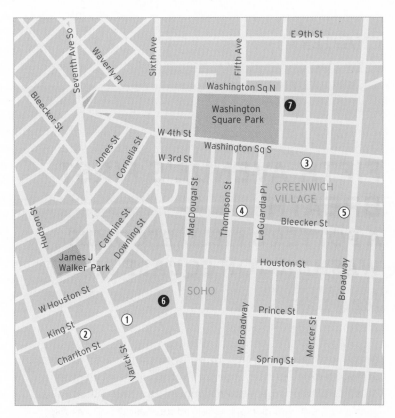

① Richmond Hill
Varick St. at Charlton St.

② Minetta Swamp
between Charlton and Houston sts.

③ Frenchtown
W 3rd and W 4th sts

④ Black and Tan Concert Hall
153 Bleecker St.

⑤ Pfaff's Beer Hall
653 Broadway

❻ Charlton-King-Vandam
Historic District

❼ New York University
100 Washington Sq. East

Key for Map
❶ Current location
⓪ Site no longer exists

CHAPTER 4

FIFTH AVENUE'S FIRST BREATH
A POTTER'S FIELD BECOMES WASHINGTON SQUARE PARK

1824–1889

Two hundred years ago, New York City smelled. Water was putrid. Garbage festered in mud. America's second-largest city—only Philadelphia was larger—was no longer a neat little Dutch village: Nearly 100,000 New Yorkers squeezed into just 17,000 low-rise buildings below Canal Street. With no urban plan to shape the unhealthy neighborhood, merchants dwelled above shops and families lived among warehouses and rowdy saloons.

As yellow fever regularly swept through town, yellow shrouds marked the bodies of those who succumbed to the disease. The bodies of the poor were buried in a nine-acre municipal square about two miles north of the settlement, amidst farmland. Today, that nine-acre potter's field is Washington Square Park, the beginning of Fifth Avenue, an international symbol of fashion and wealth.

Fifth Avenue was born in 1807, when New York's aldermen agreed to implement an urban plan. Three commissioners spent four years surveying Manhattan's hills and orchards while speculators

tried to buy up land ahead of them; landowners set dogs on them, pelted them with vegetables, and then filed the first lawsuits against the city. Eventually, those commissioners devised Manhattan's grid of 155 streets and sixteen avenues. According to the urban plan, the municipal square would serve as the base for Fifth Avenue.

From its very inception, Fifth Avenue was special. It was an elegant hundred-foot-wide boulevard for strolling, created decades before Baron Haussmann transformed Paris with its Champs-Élysées, and it provided a healthy escape from the downtown miasma. The grid plan was an early urban planning success. None of the great European capitals could boast of such efficient and disciplined use of real estate. As lots within the grid were sold, builders, residents, and services followed in logical succession, and a new city emerged from the soil.

The stretch of Fifth Avenue from the burial ground to 13th Street was opened in 1824: its land was graded and the street was paved. Cobblestones were too uneven, so city planners settled on larger Belgian blocks abutted tightly together. The curbstones—not native to the New World—were milled in England; they served as the ballast on British ships that docked regularly. Since all vehicles had iron-rimmed wheels, traffic noise roared like thunder.

The marsh at today's Washington Square became the public gallows. When the Marquis de Lafayette visited in 1824, he was treated to the sight of twenty highwaymen hanged by the neck. In 1826, the city stopped burying bodies in the square, planted some trees, paved some paths, and officially opened the Washington Military Parade Ground on July 4, 1828, in honor of the first President. But the park occasionally offered reminders of its less-than-aristocratic past when, as one Washington Square resident wrote, "the weight of heavy guns drawn over the Parade Ground crushed the tops of some of the coffins," exposing the rotted corpses below.

Although it is estimated that 25,000 bodies were decomposing beneath it, the city fathers selected Washington Square as the place to install the large well from which all Fifth Avenue residents would acquire their water. Even more amazing, those neighbors praised the water for its "clarity and softness."

With the newly organized city grid, well-heeled New Yorkers suddenly found it desirable to live apart from shops, warehouses, and saloons. Manhattan's wealthiest residents built the first Fifth Avenue houses and those along the north side of Washington Square.

The Rhinelander family, for example, had lived in New York since the 1600s as importers of china and glass, then sugar. In 1840 William Rhinelander built 14 Washington Square North at the corner of Fifth Avenue; his relatives moved into number 17. Their presence attracted other well-to-do New Yorkers, including James Lenox, who built a manse at 53 Fifth Avenue (at 12th Street). Although rich, these families lived in comfort rather than luxury, for it was fashionable to be "careful with money."

However, both families were soon speculating in New York City real estate to great success—their legacies live on in Lenox Hill and the landmark Rhinelander Mansion on Madison Avenue, now Ralph Lauren's headquarters. The families of rich businessmen soon populated all the lots "in the Fifth Avenue," with gardens in the front yard and privies in the back.

By 1893, stagecoaches were a familiar sight on Fifth Avenue, as seen in this drawing from *Harper's Magazine*

Life seemed idyllic—magnificent houses on a street with twenty-foot sidewalks, rich friends, relatives, a park, and a water source nearby. With all the shops and businesses two miles downtown, New Yorkers suddenly needed a mode of transportation. The next arrival on Fifth Avenue: stagecoaches. Even well-to-do families chose not to own a carriage, to avoid the costs of a full-time coachman, horse, and stable. Instead, starting in 1830, coaches—with six people on either side—roared up and down the avenue, and Second, Third, Sixth, and Eighth avenues as well, charging a nickel a ride. As one citizen put it: "... nowhere in America were so many fine horses to be seen. Formal coaches with high springs and double-folding steps. Indeed, Fifth Avenue was akin to a horse show."

Street life required street lamps. Gas lines were laid underground, starting in 1825. By 1847, street lamps extended all the way to 18th Street, maintained by lamplighters who switched the valves on each night with the tip of a long wand.

Next came education. When New York University opened on Washington Square East in 1831, the nearby residents were its chief donors. In the halls of higher learning, sons of those early residents were groomed to run the world. One such son, John Taylor Johnston became an executive at the Central Railroad of New Jersey, ran an art gallery, and then founded The Metropolitan Museum of Art.

Education inspired invention. Samuel Morse invented the telegraph while serving as a professor at NYU. Soon telegraph wires were strewn from giant poles throughout the city, as communication with the downtown offices took on a new immediacy. Wealthy Fifth Avenue residents installed buzzers in their houses to summon "telegraph boys" to pick up messages. The area's bucolic atmosphere began to fade as commerce encroached.

Churches followed the money, regularly relocating when residential neighborhoods turned commercial. They observed that as their congregations shrank with the influx of commerce, real estate values increased. Churches reaped profits by selling real estate (usually to be razed) in a burgeoning market, and then followed their congregants to new neighborhoods. On Sundays, churches were permitted to put chains across Fifth Avenue during services to prevent noisy stagecoaches from disrupting solemn worship.

Then Delmonico's, New York's premier restaurant, moved from William Street up to Fifth Avenue and 14th Street, bringing new excitement with it. Lower Fifth Avenue was now called the "social spine of New York" and its glory days would last from the 1830s through

University Hall at the northeast corner of the park, circa 1850 (demolished in 1894)

the 1880s. "Promenading" became a male sport. Young men, attired in the best London-made fashions, strutted with high hats, turned-up cuffs, and canes. Meanwhile, Mercer Street, just three blocks from elite Washington Square, was the main promenade for streetwalkers, with nearby taverns supporting a surprising number of brothels.

In April 1889, the city celebrated the centennial of George Washington's inauguration with a parade ending at a triumphal wooden arch spanning Fifth Avenue just 100 feet north of the square. New Yorkers from all neighborhoods were so dazzled by the temporary edifice that a permanent marble arch was installed in Washington Square to meet public demand. The completed arch was inaugurated in May 1892, commemorating the 400th anniversary of America's discovery. It was the same year that the cornerstone was laid for the Cathedral of St. John the Divine on Amsterdam Avenue at 112th Street, and just five years before Columbia University moved from 49th Street at Madison Avenue to Morningside Heights.

As the successful grid-city became as vibrant as the rowdy area below Canal Street, New Yorkers began to settle farther and farther uptown. Observing the popularity of their neighborhood—a parade route, bohemians flocking to nearby Greenwich Village, and bawdy shows on Eighth and Bleecker streets—the Fifth Avenue elite admitted the unthinkable: again, their neighborhood had begun to smell.

Parades along Fifth Avenue celebrate the centennial of George Washington's inauguration, April 1889

Turning up their noses, these stylish New Yorkers continued the city's uptown expansion.

❶ Washington Military Parade Ground

❷ Rhinelander Homes
14 Washington Sq. North
15 Washington Sq. North

③ Lenox Home
53 Fifth Ave. at 12th St.

❹ New York University
100 Washington Sq. East

⑤ Delmonico's
Fifth Ave. at 14th St.

Key for Map

❶ Current location
⓪ Site no longer exists

Fifth Avenue Style

Easter Sunday on Fifth Avenue, c. 1890, by W.T. Smedley

An afternoon lounge at Goupil's Art Gallery, Fifth Avenue and 22nd Street, 1872, in *Leslie's Illustrated Newspaper*

Ladies' drawing room in the Fifth Avenue Hotel, 1859, in *Harper's Weekly*

CHAPTER 5

FROM DYNASTY TO TRAGEDY
THE STORY OF THE ASTOR FAMILY

1783–2009

Few people believed as strongly in the viability of New York as John Jacob Astor. Barely two years after Cornwallis surrendered to George Washington, Astor immigrated to Manhattan in 1783 at the age of twenty, uneducated and barely fluent in English. With him he brought twenty-five dollars, seven German-made wooden flutes, and a wily sense of opportunism.

The son of a butcher from Waldorf, Germany, Astor started out in New York by peddling cakes in the streets for a bakery on what is now Cedar Street. When a nearby resident offered him a job at the rate of two dollars a week in the fur trade, young Astor headed up the Hudson River to Iroquois country, carrying a rifle and a sixty-pound backpack. He played his wooden flute as he traveled, often twenty miles a day, to negotiate with trappers and Indians for precious pelts, and defending his blonde scalp from hostile tribesmen. In his first year, Astor not only developed contacts in the fur trade, but also learned to navigate the forests, and identify

Mrs. Caroline Astor greets guests at her exclusive ball, 1903

America's natural resources better than most merchants.

He skillfully applied that knowledge. Profits on fur pelts were enormous, especially in Europe, where prices escalated as the American Revolution disrupted the trapping industry, causing a scarcity of pelts. Astor continued his forays into the profitable Niagara frontier, sleeping under the stars. In 1785, he married his Queen (now Pearl) Street neighbor Sarah Todd, presenting her with the seven flutes. Sarah's $300 dowry was used to import European instruments and establish her in the music business, with the front room of the Todd house (81 Queen Street) functioning as a showroom. In 1789, just five years after arriving in America, Astor retired from the musical instrument business, applying its capital to two lots on the Bowery, purchased for $625 cash. Over the next six decades, while his fur business prospered with employees across America, Astor found his greatest source of income: Manhattan real estate.

Accurately assuming that European immigration would escalate, he avoided the purchase of properties already developed, preferring farmlands he could divide into numerous lots for great profit. To them Astor applied the European concept of twenty-one-year leases, after which the property plus the tenants' improvements reverted back to him. With famine and political hardships throughout Europe, Manhattan was a boomtown. By the time Astor died in 1848, Manhattan's population increased from 25,000 residents in 1785 to 515,000. With a frantic need for more housing, Manhattan development progressed farther uptown and Astor—who owned much of the bare land upon which new homes were erected—earned the title of New York's Landlord.

With his wealth came power, which he managed from his office at 71 Liberty Street and his home at 223 Broadway near Vesey Street. Astor held the mortgage for the Greenwich Village estate of Governor DeWitt Clinton, a $75,000 investment that eventually generated $1 million annually for the Astor heirs. He even duped President Thomas Jefferson by circumventing the Embargo Act, allegedly returning a "Chinese Mandarin" to his homeland on one of

Astor's trade ships. When the boat returned to America loaded with rare teas, Astor sold his goods on the American market for $200,000, his largest transaction yet. He then used the profits to acquire all the land from Broadway to the Hudson River, from 42nd to 46th streets.

John Jacob Astor, 1794

But he wanted even more. Seeking an aristocratic title within his family, Astor arranged the marriage of his daughter Eliza to a Swiss count. He was subsequently presented to Charles X and Louis Phillippe of France, met with Prince Metternich, and attended the coronation of Ferdinand II.

Despite his conspicuous wealth, Astor was a famous miser, generous only within his family. On one of his many return visits to Waldorf, Germany, he traveled in steerage to save a few dollars. Once in Germany, however, he pensioned every relative he could locate. In New York, where one in seven residents was a pauper, he gave away nickels to children begging in the streets. When an Episcopal minister chided that Astor's philanthropy was out of scale with its potential, he switched to dimes.

In 1834, Astor built the most luxurious hotel on this continent, eventually known as Astor House. He moved his residence "uptown" to the west side of Broadway at Prince Street, sharing a business office with his son William at 85 Prince Street, and also maintaining a thirteen-acre "country estate" at Hell Gate, today's 86th to 87th streets and East End Avenue, where he entertained some of the greatest intellectuals of the era.

He befriended Aaron Burr (while also holding Burr's mortgage), Martin Van Buren, Daniel Webster, and Washington Irving, whom he regaled with stories of his colorful past. At their urging, Astor's philanthropy finally materialized in his later years. Appreciating the importance of learning, he created a library for the public at Astor Place, investing $60,000 in "curious, rare, and beautiful books." While he didn't live to see Astor Library's completion—he died in 1848, just one year before it opened—he bequeathed $400,000 toward the library building's maintenance. Today the books belong to the New York Public Library, and the building has since been reborn as The Public Theater.

Between 1820 and 1850, property values in Manhattan rose from $83 million to $286 million, of which almost $30 million belonged solely to John Jacob Astor, a staggering sum in pre-Civil War America. Responsible for much of Manhattan's earliest real estate development, the enterprising Astor rendered an unforgettable legacy, but he could not foresee the impact his great wealth would have on his heirs.

With New York City real estate investments providing steady income, Astor's grandson William Backhouse Astor, Jr. inherited the bulk of the fortune by accepting his family's plan for an arranged marriage. His bride, Caroline Webster Schermerhorn, was no great beauty, but her family had lived in New York far longer than

The Astor House hotel, Broadway between Vesey and Barclay streets

any Astor, a pedigree the family sought with vigor. Although the marriage seemed ideal to the twenty-two-year-old Caroline, twenty-three-year-old William only hung around long enough to sire four daughters and a son, but then concentrated his efforts on his millionaire playboy lifestyle. Traveling on an enormous yacht, he spent much of his time away from his family.

Mrs. Astor had other plans. With four daughters to marry off, she was determined to identify suitable partners for each of her children. In 1872, she met Ward McAllister, a Southern gentleman fascinated by New York society. Working with Mrs. Astor, who provided the money and the organizational skills, McAllister conceived the idea of a ball committee. Twenty-five prominent men—including Schermerhorns, Astors, and, of course, McAllister himself—invited five men and four ladies to every party. They became the patriarchs of New York society, controlling the very definition of who and what was fashionable.

Local publications and many tongues soon referred to Mrs. Astor as "Society's Queen" or the "Mystic Rose," dubbing McAllister as her "Prime Minister." Once their list of invitees had been established, the Balls were subscription affairs attended by the same celebrants at each gathering. Catholics and Jews were never invited to the Astor Balls. Neither were the Vanderbilts, nor the "nouveau-riche" Goulds and Harrimans. Trading on such obvious exclusions, the select list of invitees made the affairs an instant success.

As McAllister later wrote: "Applications poured in from all sides; every influence was brought to bear . . . Pressures were so great that we feared the struggle would be too fierce and engender too much rancor and bad feeling." To save face, a second string of parties, known as the Family Circle Dancing Class, was arranged to pacify the disgruntled, and included a younger set, to whom the Astor daughters might soon debut.

The renowned events took on legendary proportions. Each January, Mrs. Astor gave a ball at the family's mansion at 350 Fifth Avenue at 34th Street. Bedecked in jewels and posing under a life-size portrait of herself, Mrs. Astor greeted her guests alone.

Caroline Webster Schermerhorn Astor, 1875

As her daughters neared their debuts, McAllister and Mrs. Astor increased the attendance of the balls to 400 While Mrs. Astor explained that it was the maximum number that her ballroom could comfortably accommodate, McAllister audaciously told the press: "Why, there are only about 400 people in fashionable New York society. If you go outside that number you strike people who are either not at ease in a ballroom or else make other people not at ease."

Presenting the Astor children to the "New York 400" was a triumph, and the ballroom soon served as the site of family nuptials. In 1876, Emily Astor married James Van Alen, a dashing Civil War cavalry commander and an investor in the New York Central Railroad. In 1878, Helen Schermerhorn Astor married James Roosevelt Roosevelt, confirming ties with the powerful Roosevelt family. Soon after, Orme Wilson married Carrie Astor, with his family providing a $400,000 marriage settlement, and a distinguished guest list that included former President Ulysses S. Grant—wedding gifts reached a value of about $1 million.

Only Charlotte Astor surprised all society (and, inevitably, the press), after her marriage to James Coleman Drayton. Ten years into her marriage, and as the mother of four children, she fell in love with Hallett Alsot Borrowe, the vice president of Equitable Life, left her family and ran off to Europe with her lover. Even from his yacht in Florida, Charlotte's father William Astor was scandalized. He retaliated by writing her out of his will (although mother Caroline, who outlived her husband, made provisions to care for Charlotte years later).

That left only son John Jacob Astor IV to find his partner

in society. A lavish reception for 800 guests introduced him triumphantly in 1887. John Jacob IV married the most gentried spouse of all: Ava Lowle Willing, a descendant of Alfred the Great, Henry I, Edward I, Henry III, and Henry IV of England, and Henry I of France. (Sadly, it was this same John Jacob Astor who died on the Titanic in 1912.)

Mrs. Astor had accomplished her task, confirming the Astors as one of the most powerful families in New York, while establishing the standards by which all of society's fêtes have been measured since.

The Astor family's reputation as keepers of society lasted through the twentieth century, led by Brooke Astor, the widow of John Jacob Astor's great-grandson Vincent. The last of the Manhattan Astors, Brooke Astor died in 2007 at the age of 105. A leading social figure and philanthropist, her final years were filled with illness and mental deterioration, along with rumors of abuse and neglect at the hands of her son (from a previous marriage), Anthony Marshall.

In 2009, eighty-five-year-old Marshall was found guilty of grand larceny, having siphoned tens of millions of dollars from his mother's estate. He was sentenced to prison for up to three years, a sad end to a glittering chapter in Manhattan history.

Ballroom in Mrs. Caroline Astor and John Jacob Astor IV house, 1895, at 840 Fifth Avenue

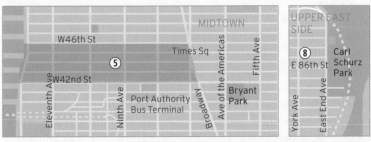

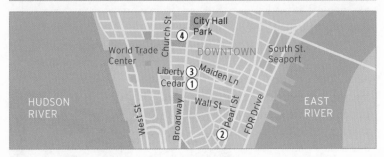

① Astor's first job
   Cedar St. Bakery

② Todd House
   81 Great Queen (now Pearl) St.

③ Astor Office
   71 Liberty St.

④ Astor Home (later the Astor House
   Hotel): Broadway between Vesey
   and Barclay sts.

❺ Astor's big buy:
   Broadway to the Hudson, from
   W. 42nd to W. 46th sts.

⑥ Astors move "Uptown"
   585 Broadway

⑦ Office of John Jacob & William Astor
   85 Prince St.

⑧ Astor Country Estate
   E. 88th St. at York Ave.

❾ Astor Library (Public Theater)
   425 Lafayette St.

⑩ William B. Astor Mansion
   350 Fifth Ave.

CHAPTER 6

A BEAR ON BROADWAY, AND A RIOT AT THE OPERA
A BRIEF HISTORY OF ASTOR PLACE

1811–1849

When the Commissioners' Plan successfully leveled all the hills and valleys in Manhattan in 1811, urban agriculture ended. Farms were replaced by row-house developments along the patterned grid of streets and avenues we know today. The expense and disruption to property owners provoked some of New York's first acts of civil disobedience, at a time when Manhattan was as wild as the West.

Broadway and the Bowery, two important commercial streets already in use, were to be extended uptown, following their existing courses. Those extensions would cross, forming a natural union at 11th Street, creating a Union Square. Hendrick Brevoort, a sixty-four-year-old descendant of early Dutch settlers, lived in the wooden house his father built on 11th Street at the Bowery. He had no intention of partitioning his land or parting with his splendid grove of trees. Learning of the planners' determination to raze the trees to make way for 11th Street, Brevoort acquired a "pet" bear, which he kept chained to a tree. Guarding his land with a blunderbuss firearm

At least twenty-five were killed during the May 10, 1849 riot at the Astor Place Opera House

James Renwick

while the bear protected the other side, Brevoort defied the Commissioners' Plan.

To this day, 11th Street meets a dead-end at Broadway, where Brevoort's grove once thrived. To avoid any altercations with Brevoort or his bear, the commissioners revised their plans for Broadway. At 10th Street, it would run parallel to the Bowery, giving us a Union Square at 14th Street, where the Bowery (now Fourth Avenue) and Broadway never meet.

When Brevoort died in 1841 at age ninety-four, his son Henry sold the grove to the Grace Church for $35,000. The trees were razed two years later by Brevoort's nephew James Renwick, a twenty-five-year-old aspiring architect who had not yet designed a single project. With Grace Church as his first commission, Renwick's career and reputation were launched, culminating in his magnificent design for St. Patrick's Cathedral a decade later.

Hendrick Brevoort's farm separates Broadway and the Bowery, 1831

Meanwhile, the elegant home of William Backhouse Astor's family stood nearby on Lafayette Place. Around the corner stood the 1,800-seat Astor Place Opera House. When an American actor, Edwin Forrest, received favorable notices for his performances on London stages, some high-minded New Yorkers thought it wise to produce *Macbeth* at the Astor Place Opera House, inviting Forrest's longtime British rival William Macready to perform. Theatergoers were furious. With wounds from the War of 1812 still too fresh in the minds of many New York veterans, Macready's appearance was a chance to fight one more battle with the British.

Grace Church on Broadway at East 11th St.

On May 10, 1849, an estimated crowd of 20,000 gathered in front of the theater, while 300 policemen escorted ticketholders inside. When Macready entered onstage as Macbeth, the theater erupted with hoots, jeers, and flying vegetables. The mob outside hurled cobblestones at the Opera House, shattering the front windows of the theater. Inside, ringleaders threw cobblestones at the theater's huge chandelier. Cut glass rained down on the audience. Meanwhile, the mob outside attacked the police. By 10 p.m., the National Guard arrived, but when guardsmen shot their firearms overhead to avoid bloodshed, the mob reached a wilder frenzy, attacking the National Guard head-on. The Colonel gave the guard orders to fire at will.

From their residence, the Astors saw the National Guard fire directly into the mob. Their theater was in shambles. The melee finally ended at 1 a.m., when the guardsmen moved two brass cannons into position. The cannons weren't used; as the sun rose, 200 protestors were wounded, and thirty-four lay dead in the street.

① Brevoort Farm
11th St. and Bowery

❷ Union Square

❸ Grace Church
802 Broadway

❹ Astor Place Opera House
425 Lafayette St.

❺ The Colonnade Row
William B. Astor's Residence
428-434 Lafayette St.

Views of Old New York

View of New York from the Hobuck Ferry House, 1800, by Francis Jukes

New York, 1851, printed by Goupil & Co.

New York with Brooklyn Bridge, after 1883

CHAPTER 7

SLUMMING
THE STORY OF FIVE POINTS
1830s–1900s

New Yorkers love to describe their city in superlatives: the biggest population, the tallest buildings, the richest millionaires, even the winning-est baseball team. What you rarely hear is the converse, though it too is true. When it comes to squalor, historic Manhattan just can't be beat, for it fostered the sleaziest, dirtiest, sickest slum in American history, just a short walk from City Hall.

The notorious slum was called Five Points. Today it only exists in the movies, most notably in Martin Scorsese's *Gangs of New York*. It's the area that partially comprises today's vibrant Chinatown, though the streets of Five Points are long gone. Imagine the era before running water, before paved streets, decades before Lincoln freed the slaves. Imagine an era when people considered it "proper" to segregate themselves by gender, by race, by religion and ethnicity. Now imagine a place where poverty is so severe that it blurs all those divisions, shocking all of "respectable" society. That was Five Points, a neighborhood packed with people desperate to

Bottle Alley and Bandit's Roost were two infamous alleyways in Mulberry Bend, the most dangerous neighborhood in all of New York, and the subject of the 1890 book *How the Other Half Lives* by Jacob Riis

Collect Pond, 1798

survive within the wooden buildings that lined the foul and muddy streets.

The place earned its name from the five corners created by several intersecting streets (where today's Worth and Baxter streets intersect, west of Mulberry Street), though the neighborhood spread for blocks in all directions. There was once a pond there, Collect Pond, and it was the neighborhood's primary attraction because water was a rare commodity on this island of solid bedrock.

When some two-and-a-half story buildings were erected near the pond a neighborhood was born. Those half-stories were usually workshops, as in the early 1800s most Americans worked with their hands. Enterprising locals became saloonkeepers; there were saloons on every block in Five Points, serving as sources for news as well as camaraderie. The unskilled laborers—many of them African-Americans who escaped slavery in the South—unloaded cargo ships in the harbor or broke rocks to clear the land.

The area declined rapidly. American cities lacked the zoning laws we take for granted today and in Five Points, residences, shops, and industries stood side-by-side. Pigs and sheep were corralled through the streets and into the local slaughterhouses; their skins were sold to tanneries. The pond that provided fresh water for residents of Five Points was the same

The Old Brewery in Five Points, 1852

pond where tanneries, breweries and slaughterhouses dumped their waste. The pond eventually became so putrid and polluted that a ditch was dug just to drain it; Canal Street was born when the pond was filled with land.

With no pond, landlords added wells and cisterns to the yards behind the tenements, far too close to their outhouses. As more immigrants crowded into the tiny rooms of Five Points, outhouses continually contaminated the water supply. As a result, cholera was a chronic illness. The stench was chronic too, but even educated people didn't make the connection. Most residents outside of Five Points simply viewed cholera as a natural condition of the "degraded" lowlifes living there. Doctors were scarce and frequently mistrusted. Residents relied on the saloons to provide their water, mixing spirits in it just to make it drinkable.

The destitution led to an unbelievable spectacle. Since there wasn't sufficient work for the rapidly increasing population, everyone learned to be a huckster of some sort, selling a service to make one day's pay stretch for a week. Prostitution was rampant; thanks to its central location, Five Points became the most popular red-light district in New York.

The Old Brewery, the neighborhood's largest and most notorious building, was converted into tiny tenement rooms. Pickpockets roamed the dark hallways and thieves stashed their booty in the windowless spaces; elsewhere, dozens of people of all

The intersection of Cross, Anthony, and Orange streets, 1827

races would sleep in a pile on each other for warmth.

The small wooden buildings were just as bad: walls were pasted over with newspapers to keep out the elements, yet landlords had no incentive to demolish these decrepit buildings, for the taxes on an old building were a fraction of what they'd pay on a new one, yet the tenancy would remain the same. Drunken brawls were a daily occurrence, spilling out into the unpaved streets. The sober ones placed bets on which drunk might prevail.

The spectacle was too enticing. In 1834, the *New York Sun* published sensational exposés, reporting "the drunkards of both sexes, intermingled with scarcely any thing to hide their nakedness, lay in a state of misery almost indescribable." That same year, Davy Crockett, Tennessee's famous frontiersman, arrived for a visit and published his observations: "Black and white, white and black, all hugemsnug together with a jug of liquor between them: and I do think I saw more drunk folks, men and women, that day, than I ever saw before." He concludes: "I would rather risque myself in an Indian fight than venture among these creatures after night . . . these are worse than savages, they are too mean to swab hell's kitchen." Davy Crockett's publication offered up Five Points' notoriety to a national audience.

In 1841, British author Charles Dickens took a swipe at the Five Points, too, writing in his *American Notes*: "Here, too, are lanes and alleys, paved with mud knee deep; underground chambers, where they dance and game; hideous tenements which take their name from robbery and murder; all that is loathsome, drooping and decaying is here." Dickens' visit was a cue to fashionable New Yorkers to go "slumming." With a police escort, wealthy visitors would arrive to gawk at the poverty on display and marvel at the vices of its residents.

Meanwhile, famine in Ireland sent extraordinary numbers of starving immigrants to America. Five Points was the inexpensive place for housing, where resourceful landlords divided wooden buildings into smaller and smaller "tenant apartments," or "tenements" for short.

Next came the Southerners, sneering that Five Points justified slavery. As one Kentucky doctor put it, Five Points' cholera patients "are far more filthy, degraded, and wretched than any slave I have beheld, under the most cruel and tyrannical master." The *Southern Quarterly Review* mused: "is [there] any negro quarter, from Mason and Dixon's line to the Rio del Norte, which could furnish a picture of vice, brutality, and degradation comparable to that drawn from the Five Points of New York?" It seemed that everyone came to judge, but few offered solutions.

The city government occasionally sprayed the streets and buildings with disinfectants, but did little to resolve the

Policemen lead upper-class tourists through the Five Points slum, 1885

Jacob Riis, c. 1900

source of the misery. Elected officials heard from temperance societies, missionaries, reformers and other do-gooders, but no one agreed on what should be done to end the wretchedness in the Five Points. When the Civil War ended and slaves were freed, African-Americans arrived in New York only to face a new kind of discrimination. While many black men learned such skills as carpentry or masonry while working in the South, those jobs were off-limits in New York. Instead, black men shoveled coal and took other menial jobs to survive; Five Points was one of the few places in which they could afford to live. It became the most densely populated neighborhood in the world, with 335,000 people per square mile circa 1888.

Right about then, the squabbling and squalor reached an abrupt end, thanks to the efforts of one lone man with a remarkable new gadget. Jacob Riis was a Danish immigrant who arrived in New York in 1870. Living a true rags-to-riches life, Riis dwelled in poorhouses, sold flatirons, and eventually landed a job as a reporter for the *New York Tribune*. For eleven years, he covered the Five Points beat, writing the brutal stories of its mean streets. Riis was also one of the first reporters to get his hands on the earliest flash attachment for a camera. It changed his career and the map of New York.

Riis left the *Tribune* in 1889 to write an eighteen-page article for *Scribner's Magazine* that included nineteen of his photographs, which were coarse, heartbreaking evidence of the lives behind the dilapidated buildings. Here were starving children in windowless rooms, looking straight into the flash of a camera. The article, famously entitled *How the Other Half Lives*, was a national sensation. Slumming lost its charm.

Next, Riis took his show on the road. He made lantern slides of his photographs, then spoke at churches and lecture halls with W. L. Craig from the Health Department. Together they articulated what no one had figured out: cholera and other diseases were not genetic afflictions of the poor. Diseases were chronic throughout Five Points because of polluted drinking water and the lack of sanitation.

Riis continued to photograph with the flash. He expanded *How the Other Half Lives* into an entire book, published in 1890. In it he delivered hard-hitting statistics such as the shocking infant mortality rate on Mulberry Street in 1888: a whopping sixty-eight percent. These harsh realities stunned the nation. Theodore Roosevelt, then head of the New York Police Board of Commissioners, arrived at Riis's office with a note that simply said: "I have read your book, and I am here to help." Riis took Roosevelt on a series of nighttime tours. Soon after, Roosevelt closed the broken-down lodging rooms and added his voice to Riis's in a call to replace the Five Points tenements.

The park at the corner of Worth Street and Baxter Street, the former Five Points intersection, opened on June 15, 1897, and is still a playground today. Although it lacks the spacious charms of Central Park, it represented a gargantuan step by city government to acknowledge the importance of light and air when designing an urban environment. Entire streets were erased as New York

Three boys sleep in the street in this photograph by Jacob Riis, 1888

reinvented the Five Points neighborhood by razing its buildings and leveling the land.

A few years later, Theodore Roosevelt, as America's twenty-sixth President, praised Jacob Riis as "the most useful citizen of New York." In that moment, he proved that in Manhattan even sad stories can end in superlatives.

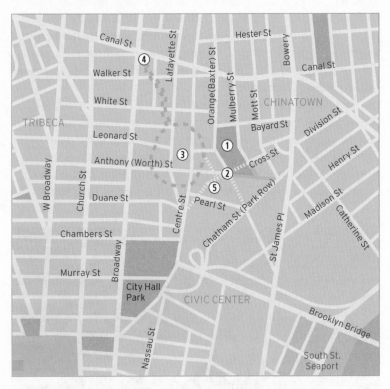

① Mulberry Bend
   (now Columbus Park)

② Five Points
   intersection of Worth and Baxter sts.
   west of Mulberry St.

③ Collect Pond

④ Ditch for Pond Drainage
   Canal St.

⑤ The Old Brewery

From Five Points to Chinatown

Chinese people didn't find their way to America in large numbers until the California Gold Rush in 1849, and many worked their way across the country on the Transcontinental Railroad. With the completion of the railroad in 1869, 30,000 men were put out of work; America's prosperity was threatened. New laws flagrantly discriminated against the Chinese: ineligible for citizenship, forbidden to marry Americans, forbidden to defend themselves in courts, even denied bail. Most hurtful of all, the U.S. Congress enacted the Chinese Exclusion Act in 1882, prohibiting all immigration from China. Women were prevented from joining their husbands, and by 1900, less than five percent of New York's Chinese population was female. "Chinese must go!" was proclaimed by politicians from all parties, while anti-Chinese legislation remained in effect until 1943.

During those sad decades, Chinese men across America were subjected to stonings, burnings, beatings, and riots that ended in murders. Union officials labeled Chinese immigrants as "the greatest danger to organized labor in America" since Chinese laborers were often hired just to cross picket lines. To escape to a safe haven, Chinese men migrated to two American cities that were famous for their tolerance: San Francisco and New York.

When the Exclusion Act became law in 1882, desperate Chinese men made Five Points their new home, the melting pot, at last. Generations of Irish immigrants who once populated the place were now inching their way

into the middle class and out of the poor neighborhood. Chinese bachelors took their place.

From the cruel treatment they'd experienced elsewhere in America, these Chinese men realized that to live safely in America, they needed to be self-sufficient. Two types of businesses flourished: laundries and restaurants. In these industries, no one could claim that Chinese laborers were taking work away from American citizens. That's how Chinatown was born.

Today, Manhattan's Chinatown is still famous for its proliferation of restaurants, but the cultural mix is changing. While its earliest Chinese settlers were primarily Cantonese, new dialects are taking over Chinatown as immigrants arrive from other provinces, finding comfort in familiar sounds and smells.

Meanwhile, the neighborhood is undergoing yet another transformation, as a new wave of restaurants, boutiques, and art galleries bring a youthful energy to this old-school New York neighborhood.

CHAPTER 8

MANHATTAN'S INCANDESCENCE
THOMAS EDISON ELECTRIFIES NEW YORK

1880–1882

Inventor Thomas Edison invited New York City's aldermen to his New Jersey laboratory on January 2, 1880, served them champagne and a catered feast, then proudly presented his latest invention: the incandescent lamp. Here was steady, brilliant illumination, a major improvement over gaslight's irregularly flickering flames. The aldermen balked.

Thrilled by his own ingenuity, Edison recommended that city funds be spent to string electric wires throughout Manhattan, placing his new invention on every street corner. The aldermen groaned: Sure, the light bulb was an impressive gimmick, but why give up New York's beautiful gaslights? Corruption was legendary, and politicians regularly sold their allegiances to the highest bidder. Since the mayor firmly backed the gas companies, the aldermen viewed Edison with caution. Manhattan's skyline was already marred by drooping telegraph wires, telephone wires, and stock tickers, which the Board of Aldermen now used against

Thomas Alva Edison, 1878

Edison to intentionally hamper his progress. They passed a law prohibiting him from installing electrical wires overhead anywhere in New York. Their message to Edison was plain: Don't mess with the gas companies. Instead, the city continued to pay a small army of lamplighters fifty cents a month for each lamp they maintained, with each route including up to 100 lamps per night.

Unfazed, Edison displayed his light bulb to private users. He recognized, two years earlier, that if he was to perfect an electric light bulb, he would need control of the electrical source first. With J. P. Morgan's investment bank handling the finances, he formed the Edison Electric Light Company, selling shares to New York's most prominent industrialists, including railroad tycoon W. H. Vanderbilt, Western Union director Hamilton Twombly, and others.

J. P. Morgan was among the richest men in New York. He saw the potential impact of Edison's bold new gadget, and the windfall that would surely accompany it. When Morgan retained Edison's company to install electric lights throughout his home at 219 Madison Avenue (at 36th Street), the race was on. While there are no written records as to what swayed the aldermen, on April 19, 1881, over the objections of the mayor, but with the muscle of Morgan and the Vanderbilts, Edison was granted official use of one square mile of Lower Manhattan's streets for the purpose of installing underground electrical conduits.

Following J. P. Morgan's endorsement, investors clamored for the new lighting systems. Edison bought 255-257 Pearl Street for $150,000, installed six electrical generators, and began the costly process of digging up Manhattan's unpaved streets and embedding the conduits that would one day carry electricity.

He opened a school at 65 Fifth Avenue, where The New School currently stands, to teach his employees about electricity. Meanwhile, the suspicious Commissioner of Public Works, another friend of the gas lobby, assigned five full-time inspectors to observe the labors of Edison's installers, demanding that Edison pay each of them the exorbitant salary of five dollars per day. (In 1881, many New Yorkers were earning five dollars for a sixty-hour work week.)

With not a single bulb in operation, investors still flocked to Edison. By opening new electrical companies in several neighborhoods, Edison sold shares of stock to meet the growing demands of additional investors. By October 1, 1881, he had strung wires into the buildings of fifty-nine customers. His stock, which had a face value of $100, soared, sometimes advancing by $100 an hour. It rose to $500, then $5,000, then $8,000.

Finally on September 4, 1882, thirty-five-year-old Edison invited investors, scientists, and journalists to J. P. Morgan's opulent bank at 23 Wall Street to watch the lights come on. It was chief electrical engineer John Lieb who put the massive Pearl Street generators in motion just before 3 p.m. Tension rose as the assembled guests alternately watched the unlit lamps, the emotional Edison, and the hands of the clock as they swept toward three. A minute before 3 p.m., one of Morgan's directors cried out: "A hundred dollars the lights don't go on."

"Taken!" Edison shouted back. Then he turned the switch, bringing all 106 lights in Morgan's office to life in one historic gesture. That same day, electricity was delivered to eighty-five Manhattan addresses wired with 400 light bulbs, including some prominent shops on Nassau Street, and fifty-two lamps in the editorial room of the *New York Times* at 41 Park Row. As dusk descended, Manhattan was illuminated. A *Times* article described the noteworthy product the following day: "The light was more

The Madison Avenue home of J. P. Morgan, the first New York residence wired for electricity

brilliant than gas and a hundred times steadier . . . with no nauseous smell, no flicker, no glare."

Within fourteen months, Edison's companies provided service to 508 subscribers with 12,732 bulbs. The need for his product was immediately apparent, to the collective dismay of the mayor, the aldermen, the employees and shareholders of New York's six gas companies. For decades, whenever a light bulb burned out, a technician from Thomas Edison's company was summoned to the site to perform the scientific task of changing a light bulb, and it was well into the twentieth century before all of New York was wired for electricity.

Edison announced his goal, to "make electric light so cheap that only the rich will be able to burn candles." In the process, Edison's remarkable achievements gave birth to two companies that today's New Yorkers know well. The light bulb manufacturing company became General Electric in 1883. The electric companies Edison established in various neighborhoods were eventually merged into one entity: Consolidated Edison, today's Con Ed, the original mass provider of electricity.

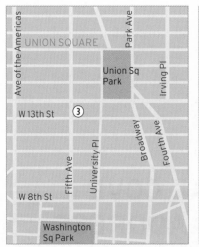

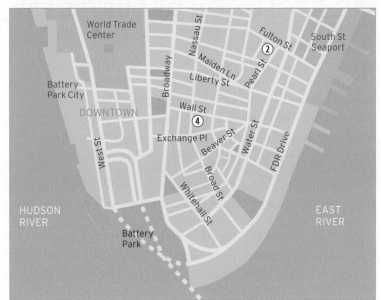

❶ Home of J. P. Morgan
219 Madison Ave.

❷ Edison's Electrical Generators
255-257 Pearl St.

③ Edison's School
65 Fifth Ave.

④ J.P. Morgan's Bank
23 Wall St.

CHAPTER 9

FROM DEUTAL COVE TO COVETED ADDRESS
THE EVOLUTION OF TURTLE BAY

1639–2001

Some Manhattan neighborhoods seem to coalesce spontaneously: SoHo, NoHo, West Chelsea, and TriBeCa grew in response to Manhattan's tight housing market, their dwellings created within commercial facades. Meanwhile, other neighborhoods have been residential since before New York City was a city.

Consider Turtle Bay—the area defined roughly as 43rd Street to 53th Street, between Lexington Avenue to the East River. This bay was actually a marsh that formed a cove between East 41st to 48th streets, the present site of the United Nations. Water trickled into it from a spring at the southeast corner of today's Central Park. The cove proved useful to seafaring vessels during the Revolutionary War in 1776, and to Robert Fulton, who tested his steam-powered boats there in 1808. But by the 1860s, the bay was covered with landfill.

Where are the turtles? Not in Turtle Bay, surprisingly. The area earned its name when, in 1639, the Dutch governor of New

Amsterdam permitted two Englishmen to settle there after they were captured. The original land grant referred to the property as "Deutal," the Dutch word for a bent blade, in reference to the shape of the land. In 1664, when the British captured New Amsterdam, "Deutal Bay" was anglicized into Turtle Bay, the name it's had ever since.

The land was divided into two farms. To the south, Turtle Bay Farm was owned by Sir Peter Warren, a British Naval Officer who was later buried with honors in Westminster Abbey. His neighbor to the north was James Beekman, a notorious Revolutionary patriot who built a mansion near 51st Street and First Avenue, which he named Mount Pleasant. The British occupied this mansion during the Revolutionary War, using its greenhouse for the trial and sentencing of patriot Nathan Hale in 1776. One day later, near the Dove Tavern at Third Avenue and 66th Street, Hale uttered his famous last words: "I only regret that I have but one life to lose for my country."

While the two farms were divided into blocks and lots in 1830, Beekman's high ground overlooking the river remained an estate. His nephew, James W. Beekman, became a distinguished New York state senator who developed the property by grading the streets and adding water mains to attract new neighbors, including Horace Greeley, publisher of the *New York Tribune*, who bought seven acres between 48th and 49th streets.

Conversely, Sir Peter Warren's daughters developed Turtle Bay Farm more haphazardly, without restricting the land along the river to residential use; carpentry shops, match factories and breweries filled the dead-end streets. Squatters built shanties at East 42nd Street and a foul-smelling slaughterhouse became First Avenue's prominent new fixture.

Residences were developed in earnest following the Civil War, with brownstones soon lining most streets. After standing for over 100 years, Mount Pleasant was torn down in 1874, although parts of the house and its furnishings are preserved by the New-York Historical Society. Horse cars on Second and Third avenues caused

The Beekman house at 50th Street and First Avenue

such congestion that the former property lines of the Beekman and Turtle Bay farms were forgotten. A new kind of divider had arrived: the elevated railway.

The Third Avenue Railroad line opened in 1878 and the Second Avenue line opened in 1880. Although they provided vital communication and rapid transit to a booming city, these railroads compromised Turtle Bay. Sunshine on the wide boulevards was blocked by shadow, and marred by soot and noise, the dingy avenues were filled by pawnshops, bars, and cheap apartments. The proud brownstones to the east of the train tracks became an ever more secluded neighborhood.

By 1900, deterioration overtook those eastside brownstones. Many were divided into inexpensive rooming houses for transient tenants. Throngs of European immigrants subdivided Turtle Bay into ethnic neighborhoods: Italians to the east of Second Avenue, Irish and Germans to the west, while 49th to 51st streets were largely Jewish. East 48th Street became home to transient actors, musicians, and stagehands. By the end of the First World War, Turtle Bay meant low rent.

The Third Avenue Railroad, which ran until 1955

In 1919, the townhouses of Turtle Bay were "rediscovered." Mrs. Walton Martin envisioned a group of townhouses surrounding a communal garden as she had seen in Italy. She assembled twenty contiguous houses; ten on 49th Street and ten behind them on 48th Street, then reconfigured the adjacent gardens to include a central path and common garden, including a fountain like the one at Villa de Medici in Florence. Following their renovations, the exciting new attraction of "Turtle Bay Gardens" brought attention and revitalization to the entire vicinity.

Powerful residents moved in, including Katharine Hepburn, Tyrone Power, Ruth Gordon and Garson Kanin, Mary Martin, and Leopold Stokowski. Avenue A was renamed Sutton Place, in honor of Effingham B. Sutton, a neighborhood merchant during the 1880s. Soon Beekman Place, Sutton Place, and the adjacent blocks underwent restorations as well, through the efforts of J. P. Morgan's daughter Anne, Theodore Roosevelt's son Kermit, and Mrs. William K. Vanderbilt.

Next came developers with even grander dreams. Fred French planned a "city within a city" for Turtle Bay. In just thirty-five days, he purchased all the buildings between First and Second Avenue, from 40th to 43rd streets, a five-acre assemblage that cost him $7.5 million. In 1928, he opened "Tudor City," twelve magnificent new buildings housing 7,500 people. It brought the neighborhood its own post office, monthly magazine, and landscaped park. Its architects succeeded in blocking the offensive odors from the First Avenue slaughterhouses by facing all living rooms to the west, with back corridors overlooking the river.

The Second Avenue Railroad was torn down between 1940 and 1942. In 1955, the Third Avenue Railroad was demolished, returning Second and Third avenues to cleanliness and light. Once the neighborhood gasped fresh air, it promptly erupted with celebrity. In elegant apartment houses like One Beekman Place and the restored townhouses nearby, Greta Garbo, Cole Porter, Ethel Barrymore, Billy Rose, Lillian Gish, Irving Berlin, Henry Luce, Efrem Zimbalist, Dame Judith Anderson, and other prominent New Yorkers proudly made Turtle Bay their home. In 1946, John D. Rockefeller, Jr. added more luster to Turtle Bay when he acquired all the riverfront property from 42nd to 48th streets—including the pungent slaughterhouses and breweries—by paying $8.5 million to developer William Zeckendorf. When the U.S. Congress passed a special statute exempting the Rockefellers from gift tax, all property and waterfront rights were conveyed to build the United Nations.

Today, Turtle Bay's past lives side-by-side with modern development. In 2001 Donald Trump opened his World Tower on First Avenue; its seventy-two stories reach the height of a ninety-story building. With Trump's bold statement, the landfill over "Deutal" cove began its next lofty chapter.

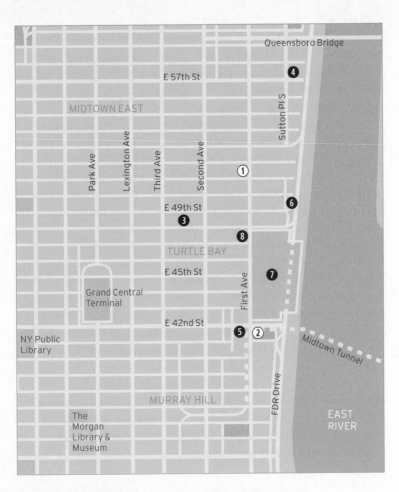

① Beekman mansion, Mount Pleasant
   E. 51st St. at First Ave.

② Shanties of Corcoran's Roost
   First Ave. and E. 42nd St.

❸ Turtle Bay Gardens

❹ Sutton Place

❺ Tudor City

❻ One Beekman Place

❼ United Nations

❽ Trump World Tower

Key for Map

⓿ Current location

⓪ Site no longer exists

CHAPTER 10

THE GOLD COAST
FIFTH AVENUE MOVES UPTOWN
1824–

As soon as the first blocks of Fifth Avenue were paved from
Washington Square to 13th Street in 1824, Manhattan's wealthiest
businessmen built splendid new homes for their families, escaping
the mud and disease of Lower Manhattan. But they faced a big
surprise, for their new neighborhood wasn't bucolic for long. The
cluster of prominent names within those few streets drew attention
to the important new address, forever defining Fifth Avenue by its
occupants' wealth.

Meanwhile, down on Beaver Street in 1827, two Swiss brothers
opened Manhattan's trendiest restaurant: Delmonico's, soon the
most popular French restaurant in New York. Learning the addresses
of their wealthiest patrons, the Delmonico brothers attempted a
radical move in 1861: They left lower Manhattan to relocate right
on Fifth Avenue itself, at the northeast corner of 14th Street, just
beyond the famed residences. Delmonico's grand new address
bestowed instant prestige; its ballrooms and dining rooms were the

scenes of countless gatherings of wealth and fashion. Samuel Morse, the inventor of Morse code and a professor at nearby New York University, even telegraphed the first intercontinental cablegram from his table in Delmonico's grand ballroom.

Prestige was conferred outdoors too, as large-scale projects gained public acceptance when displayed on Fifth Avenue. Gaslights soon lined the sidewalks all the way past 50th Street. Stagecoaches roared up and down the two-way avenue in four-minute intervals. In 1842, the city's massive aqueducts were completed, finally pumping millions of gallons of fresh water into the Croton Reservoir at Fifth Avenue and 42nd Street, where the water was distributed directly into the expensive townhouses down Fifth Avenue. Decorated like an Egyptian temple, the reservoir was an important destination for a Sunday stroll, as visitors climbed its stairs to a forty-foot summit, then strolled around the perimeter. As Edgar Allan Poe wrote in the *Broadway Journal*, "You can see from this elevation the whole city to the Battery, with a large portion of the harbor and long reaches of the Hudson and East Rivers."

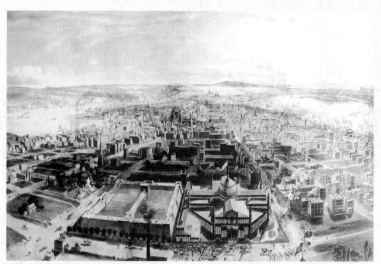

City view from 42nd Street, Croton Reservoir and Crystal Palace to the south, William Wellstood, 1855

With Delmonico's commercial precedent on Fifth Avenue at 14th Street, other businesses eagerly catered to Manhattan aristocrats on their home turf. The blocks between 14th Street to 23rd Street attracted hotels, clubs, and businesses as the avenue expanded northward. Foreign royalty arrived to experience Fifth Avenue, too. The Fifth Avenue Hotel, at 23rd Street, hosted such visitors as the Prince of Wales, the Prince of Siam, Prince Napoleon, and the last emperor of Brazil. It's where politicians conceived their plans to make a president of Ulysses S. Grant and a vice president of Theodore Roosevelt; where celebrities like Mark Twain, former president Chester A. Arthur, and actor Edwin Booth made their New York homes. Nearby, the Victoria Hotel became President Grover Cleveland's New York home between his terms in office, at 27th Street.

The foreign press was impressed, too. When it came to wonders like hot running water indoors, British reporter Edward Dicey gushed in 1863, "All the domestic arrangements are wonderfully perfect." However, when reviewing the celebrated residents of Fifth Avenue, they sneered. In London, Anthony Trollope wrote: "I know no great man, no celebrated statesman who has lived on Fifth Avenue. That gentleman on the right made a million dollars by inventing a shirt collar; the one on the left electrified the world by a lotion. Such are the aristocracy of Fifth Avenue."

To proud Fifth Avenue millionaires, there was only one solution: build bigger. If the accomplishments of America's millionaires couldn't earn them acceptance among the old money crowd overseas, then they would dazzle the world by flaunting even greater wealth than crowned royalty. Comforted by American ingenuity and spectacular wealth, the Fifth Avenue gentry knew how to surpass the luxurious lifestyles of those titled Europeans. Pouring their fortunes from private industries into Manhattan real estate, they speculated on the building boom throughout the city, as boatloads of people arrived each day to live in New York.

Then came the Gold Coast: extraordinary mansions in the middle of America's most urban city, filled with the latest amenities

Delmonico's at 44th Street, 1903

and the best European antiques that Americans could ship back home. Once-sedate residents of lower Fifth Avenue embraced grand new lifestyles, vaunting their wealth through the magnificent facades of homes they built farther up the avenue.

They faced hurdles, too. Who would want to live within the commercial stretch between 14th and 23rd streets? Not Mrs. William Backhouse Astor, for example, who shunned lower Fifth Avenue to establish a house uptown at 34th Street. Other great names soon built grand homes north of 23rd Street.

The Delmonico brothers heard the warning cry and knew it was time to move their operation yet again. If their wealthiest patrons were moving across 23rd Street, so would they. In 1876, Delmonico's lavish new restaurant opened at 26th Street. It soon faced another hurdle: a wild new dessert called ice cream was the rage, and Louis Sherry's restaurant on Fifth Avenue at 37th Street was the best place to find it. Competition was everywhere, in Fifth Avenue's businesses as well as residences.

No one was content with last year's opulence, moving farther uptown into more elaborate structures. To residents, this guaranteed good seats at the opera, membership in exclusive men's clubs, which also abandoned their roots below 23rd Street, and of course, the best tables at the best restaurants.

So, the Vanderbilts left Washington Square for a new house on Fifth Avenue at 51st Street. Even P. T. Barnum built a residence beyond the reservoir at 438 Fifth Avenue. Fifth Avenue businesses followed their wealthy patrons. When Sherry's Hotel moved to Fifth Avenue at 44th Street, champagne flowed as the celebrated clientele packed the place. Delmonico's faced down their competition by

Dinner celebrating the 70th birthday of Mark Twain (second from left), Delmonico's, 1905

relocating directly across the street. Together, they prospered until Prohibition shut them both down.

The next generation of Vanderbilts erected a mansion at 57th Street, then scored the ultimate coup—a royal title—when their daughter married a European Count. Meanwhile, as the result of a family feud, Mrs. Astor built a mansion at 65th Street, facing the new Central Park. (The feud also resulted in a pair of competing hotels, The Waldorf and the Astoria, on the sites where two Astor mansions once stood at Fifth Avenue and 34th Street.)

And so it went. Developing Fifth Avenue became a fierce *Monopoly* game. In an era when the average worker earned twelve dollars for a sixty-hour workweek, New York's capitalists and entrepreneurs demolished million-dollar homes and built them again uptown to impress the neighbors.

The Gold Coast Today

Later generations of New York's wealthiest families sold the choice sites of their childhood homes to reap even greater profits from apartment house construction. However, thanks to philanthropic efforts, several remarkable Gold Coast mansions from this era survive today.

Henry Clay Frick once controlled the largest coke and steel operation in the world. Carrère and Hastings designed his house at One East 70th Street, which now holds the revered Frick Collection.

James B. Duke's family earned its fortune in tobacco, building several Fifth Avenue residences. His daughter Doris Duke gave their final mansion at One East 78th Street to New York University for its Institute of Fine Arts.

The Whitney family earned a fortune from railroads and Standard Oil. Their former residence at 972 Fifth Avenue near 79th Street now houses the Cultural Services of the French Embassy.

The final home of Mrs. Cornelius Vanderbilt III was designed by Carrère and Hastings. It stands at the southeast corner of 86th Street and Fifth Avenue, and is occupied today by the Neue Galerie museum for German and Austrian art.

Andrew Carnegie invested his legendary wealth from the Pennsylvania Railroad and steel mills into a mansion so grand that passersby soon called the entire vicinity Carnegie Hill in deference to his imposing residence. It stood at 2 East 91st Street, where the Cooper-Hewitt, National Design Museum of the Smithsonian Institution now resides.

❶ Henry Clay Frick Residence
  (Frick Collection)
  One East 70th St.

❷ James B Duke Residence
  (Institute of Fine Arts)
  One East 78th St.

❸ Whitney Residence
  (Cultural Services of the
  French Embassy)
  972 Fifth Ave.

❹ Cornelius Vanderbilt III Residence
  (Neue Galerie)
  86th St. at Fifth Ave.

❺ Andrew Carnegie Residence
  (Cooper-Hewitt Museum)
  2 East 91st St.

⑥ Delmonico's (1862)
  One East 14th St.

⑦ Croton Reservoir (1842)
  Fifth Ave. at 42nd St.

⑧ Fifth Avenue Hotel (1858)
  Fifth Ave. at 23rd St.

⑨ Victoria Hotel (1868)
  Fifth Ave. at 27th St.

⑩ William B. Astor Jr., Residence (1862) 350 Fifth Ave. at 34th St.

⑪ Delmonico's (1876) Fifth Ave. at 26th St.

⑫ Louis Sherry's (1890) Fifth Ave. at 37th St.

⑬ William Henry Vanderbilt Mansion (1882) Fifth Ave. at 51st St.

⑭ P. T. Barnum Mansion (1867) 438 Fifth Ave.

⑮ Tiffany & Co. (1870) Union Sq. West at 15th St.

⑯ Tiffany & Co.: Fifth Ave (1905) 409 Fifth Ave. at 37th St.

⑰ Sherry's Hotel (1898) Fifth Ave. at 44th St.

⑱ Delmonico's (1896) Fifth Ave. at 44th St.

⑲ Cornelius Vanderbilt II Mansion (1882) One West 57th St.

⑳ Mrs. Astor's House (1893) Fifth Ave. at 65th St.

CHAPTER 11

PARK AVENUE
THE FROG PRINCE
1872–1905

There was a time when Park Avenue was known as Fourth Avenue, and it was populated mainly by breweries, factories, and small farms. Its most notable features were the noisy, filthy trains that ran down two tracks at its center, all the way to Prince Street. An unfortunate ridge of stone, the schist into which many of Manhattan's skyscrapers are embedded, put opposing sides of the avenue at uneven elevation through much of upper Manhattan, making real estate development impractical. Railroad entrepreneur Cornelius Vanderbilt provided a few iron walkways above the tracks for pedestrians, but crossing Fourth Avenue in a carriage was simply impossible in much of upper Manhattan.

Meanwhile, Vanderbilt pocketed a fortune. With more than thirty trains, his railroad transported about 8,000 passengers daily. However, popular sentiment turned against him when two locomotives exploded and burned below 14th Street. Outraged politicians demanded that locomotive power cease within the

"populated" areas of the city, triggering a series of legal precedents. For the very first time, American lawmakers contemplated the regulation of privately owned businesses that "affect the public interest," eventually reaching the U.S. Supreme Court. Vanderbilt complied by stopping his locomotives at his 42nd Street depot, hitching horses to his occupied passenger cars, then hauling his customers to their downtown destinations.

Reformers demanded more. Observing that upper Manhattan's expansion was hampered by the railroad, reformers rallied for the trains to be enclosed in sunken tunnels. To Cornelius, two tracks down Fourth Avenue just weren't enough anymore. In 1872, Vanderbilt purchased the craggy promontory along Fourth Avenue for an astonishingly low price, in exchange agreeing to blast the stone, level the grade of the avenue in the process, and bury his four tracks, which would emerge above ground at 97th Street. His $6.5 million project cost almost $75,000 per block. Ironically, a few months later, an unrelated financial panic hit Wall Street, closing the Stock Exchange for ten days. Businesses went bankrupt, men were suddenly out of work, and Cornelius Vanderbilt easily assembled a workforce of 2,500 men, as laborers clamored for employment.

Grand Central Station, 1900

By 1875, the project was complete. The Avenue was now 140 feet wide, the grandest boulevard in New York, with fifteen-foot sidewalks, and a fifty-six-foot wide center mall providing relief and ventilation from the not-so-grand fumes, filth, and deafening noise from the tunnel below. With the grade now level, once-mercenary Vanderbilt was viewed as a visionary who provided a spectacular service to the city, and residential real estate development became a possibility above 42nd Street all along Fourth Avenue.

When Vanderbilt died two years later in 1877, he was recognized for shortening the New York-to-Chicago travel-time from fifty hours to twenty-four, and for establishing mass transit as a reliable form of transportation within New York City.

Cornelius Vanderbilt

In March 1888, the City Aldermen agreed to rename the boulevard Park Avenue. It took a while for society's royalty to accept Park Avenue; its development is solely a twentieth-century phenomenon. It wasn't until September 1906, when the trains were electrified—minimizing the noise and reducing the need for ventilation—that the malls of Park Avenue could be landscaped. Today, the Vanderbilt legacy continues on Park Avenue. St. Bartholomew's Church, located at Park Avenue and 50th Street, boasts a trio of bronze doors designed by Stanford White and dedicated to the Vanderbilts. Like Fifth Avenue, the first important residences to be erected on the new Park Avenue were not the magnificent apartment houses we revere today; they were one-family mansions for wealthy, powerful New Yorkers.

One of the first and most prominent mansions was erected in 1905 at East 71st Street, the home of Secretary of State Elihu Root, designed by Carrère and Hastings. The *Real Estate Record* commented that Root "built a handsome house, and the result has been to improve the character and tone of the neighborhood . . .

The sunken track of the N.Y. and Harlem Railroad, Fourth Avenue, 1876

which fact alone will make the section a fashionable and restricted quarter for many years to come."

Mansions on Park Avenue

Some terrific mansions still stand on Park Avenue, though their days as private residences appear to be over. Some converts:

680 Park, designed by McKim, Mead & White, was formerly the residence of Percy Pyne, but later became the Soviet Mission to the United Nations. Its second-floor balcony was the site of two much-publicized press conferences held by Premier Nikita Khrushchev in 1962. It was later purchased by a granddaughter of John D. Rockefeller, who donated it to the Center for Inter-American Relations.

686 Park, the former home of William Douglas Sloane, head of the

W & J Sloane furniture and carpet stores, was sold in 1959 to become the Italian Cultural Institute.

690 Park, built for Henry Pomeroy Davison, a founder of Bankers Trust, then later a partner of J.P. Morgan, was sold along with 52 East 69th Street in 1955, to become the Italian Consulate.

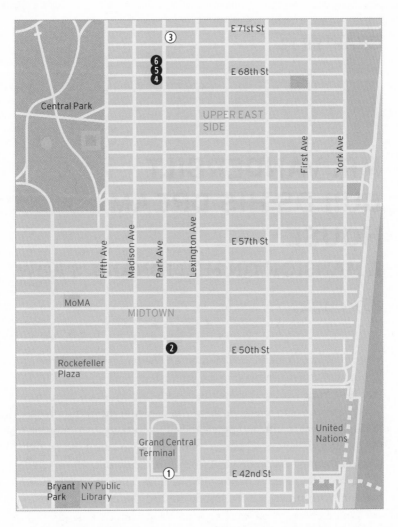

① Vanderbilt's 42nd St. Train Depot

② St. Bartholomew's Church
109 East 50th St.

③ Elihu Root's Mansion
733 Park Ave.

④ Percy Pyne Mansion: 680 Park Ave.
(Americas Society)

⑤ William Douglas Sloane Mansion
686 Park Ave. (Italian Cultural
Institute)

⑥ Henry Pomeroy Davison Mansion
690 Park Ave. (Italian Consulate)

CHAPTER 12

MR. VANDERBILT BUILDS HIS DREAM HOUSE
A MANSION ON MILLIONAIRE'S ROW

1879–1927

When it comes to marvelous Manhattan residences, no modern-day fantasy can measure up to the astonishing reality of post-Civil War New York. During the late nineteenth century, when immense fortunes were being amassed, there was no better means by which to display great wealth and proclaim self-importance than through the public spectacle of a Manhattan mansion. No one, it seems, did it better than the descendents of Cornelius Vanderbilt, who erected no less than four resplendent mansions along Fifth Avenue between 52nd and 57th streets, a stretch soon dubbed "Millionaire's Row."

One such grandson was Cornelius Vanderbilt II. Blessed with a stunning fortune, "Corneil" and his wife Alice observed that fashionable society was moving uptown, away from the 14th Street thoroughfare and the Astor mansion at 34th Street. In 1879, at age thirty-eight, Corneil acquired two brownstones at the corner of Fifth Avenue and 57th Street, then demolished them. He hired George Post, the only architect who was regularly invited to Mrs. Astor's

Cornelius Vanderbilt II by John Singer Sargent, 1890

"New York 400" balls, to design the Vanderbilt dream house at One West 57th Street.

Inspired by the Château de Blois in the Loire Valley of France, built of red bricks and limestone, Post's design for the mansion included turrets, bays, and a huge mansard roof with multiple gables. The sumptuous interior boasted Corneil's important art collection, including works by Henri Rousseau, Jean-Baptiste-Camille Corot, Jacob van Ruisdael, and J. M. W. Turner, among others. He retained John LaFarge, the renowned decorative artist, to create the stained glass windows and sculptured ceilings, while Augustus Saint-Gaudens created the sculptural staircases and Karl Bitter embellished the paneling. Inlays of gold, silver, ivory, and pearls were everywhere. New York's newest mansion was also its most chic private museum. As a monument to the power and achievement of the Vanderbilts, the edifice was an enormous success.

The Vanderbilt mansion heralded the emergence of imperial America. Here was a family lacking royal blood, yet its wealth and prestige rivaled any noble house in Europe. The Vanderbilt mansion confirmed the limitless possibilities of the New World; it captured the imaginations of people everywhere.

From its construction in 1881, the Vanderbilt mansion was a tourist attraction. The passengers of every carriage on Fifth Avenue knew when they were passing the home of Alice and Cornelius Vanderbilt II. Yet those within the Vanderbilts' social circle were less impressed. Montgomery Schuyler in the *Architectural Record* sneered: "A sad botch, incident to a reaching desire after imposing effect." After a few gala social functions, Alice and Corneil had to

The Vanderbilt Mansion at Fifth Avenue and 57th Street, 1908

admit that they too had envisioned something better. Their beautiful first-floor drawing rooms were no substitute for a real ballroom. If they were to entertain on the epic scale that befitted their social prominence, they needed a bigger house.

Back came architect George Post, this time in concert with Richard Morris Hunt, while Louis Tiffany served as interior designer.

Corneil purchased and demolished the four remaining brownstones on Fifth Avenue, then built a new facade that adjoined the manse at 4 West 58th Street, facing Grand Army Plaza and Central Park. While the original mansion cost a staggering $750,000 to construct, the new addition and renovation cost an extra $3 million, as crews worked around the clock, often under giant electric lights. Even with 800 laborers, construction took two years. The Vanderbilts got their ballroom, along with a porte cochere (a covered driveway that enabled guests to enter without fear of rain or mud), massive fireplaces, boiseries (finely detailed architectural carvings, sometimes called "gingerbread") and ormolu (molded brass fittings, often applied onto marble). Upon its completion, the

Cornelius Vanderbilt II with Mayor William Jay Gaynor and Theodore Roosevelt (standing), 1910

Vanderbilt dream house was the largest private residence in America.

However, even among Vanderbilts, dreams don't always manifest themselves according to plan. Eldest son William died of typhoid at age twenty-two, but not before introducing his younger brother Neily to Miss Grace Graham Wilson, a beautiful and worldly debutante. Three years later, when Grace turned up again, on the arm of Neily Vanderbilt, Corneil and Alice recognized the real cost of making a public spectacle of their wealth. They perceived Miss Wilson as a social climber, out to marry a Vanderbilt, any Vanderbilt.

In Paris, Neily pledged his devotion to Grace, and Corneil traveled to Europe, threatening to exclude Neily from his will.

The press on two continents had a field day following the domestic entanglements of America's richest star-crossed lovers. In July 1896, Corneil banished Neily from One West 57th Street; days later he was felled by a stroke. All of America wondered if death would again visit the Vanderbilt dream house. With his father on his deathbed, Neily married Grace in her family's mansion at 608 Fifth Avenue in August 1896, which the press reported as the wedding that cost Neily $60 million, since disinheritance seemed inevitable. When Corneil died of a cerebral hemorrhage in 1899, he was only fifty-six years old. True to his word, Corneil's last will, dated on Neily's wedding day, bequeathed $42 million to younger son Alfred, while Neily was given $500,000.

The saddest part came next. Alice inherited the dream house, filled with treasures she and Corneil barely had the chance to enjoy. For twenty-six more years, Alice resided there, seldom entertaining, haunted by her memories. Hotels, shops, offices, and overwhelming noise soon enveloped her now-too-public home. In 1920, the real estate taxes alone cost $130,000; it was time to part with the dream house. That's when Alice faced another crushing reality: no one in twentieth-century America could afford to live like a nineteenth-century Vanderbilt. She waited for years and finally acquiesced to the Braisted Realty Corp., an organization that saw little romance in the dream house. It paid $7.1 million just to get the land and knock it down.

But first, in one last gloriously sentimental gesture, Alice invited the public to tour the house for one week in January 1926. The fifty-cent admission fees were donated to charity. Movie theater baron Marcus Loew bought fragments of the house that he installed in various Loew's theaters across America, including the giant Tiffany chandelier from the Moorish room, which went into the foyer of the Loew's State Theater in Syracuse.

In 1927, Fifth Avenue lost one of its most splendid landmarks: Vanderbilt's dream house was razed. The painted ceilings, the mirrored walls, the massive staircases, the carvings, and the mantles were all smashed into rubble and hauled off to a New Jersey landfill. Corneil's daughter Gertrude Whitney, founder of the Whitney Museum, paid to remove the imposing wrought-iron gates, which are now at the entrance of the Conservatory Garden in Central Park. The Saint-Gaudens fireplace from the entry hall, and some of the glasswork by John LaFarge are all that remain of the interior. You can view them today in the American Wing of The Metropolitan Museum of Art.

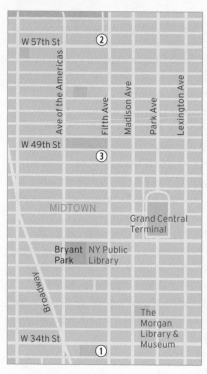

① Astor Mansion
Fifth Ave. at 34th St.

② Vanderbilt Dream House
One West 57th Street

③ Family Home of Grace Graham Wilson
608 Fifth Ave.

④ Conservatory Garden
in Central Park

⑤ Metropolitan Museum of Art
1000 Fifth Ave.

Key for Map
❶ Current location
① Site no longer exists

CHAPTER 13

DOWN THE MIDDLE
CENTRAL PARK,
AND HOW IT GOT THAT WAY

1851–1866

"A miracle in the middle of Manhattan!" is the way one tour guide describes Central Park. But the real miracle is that this urban oasis even exists, for the dramatic story of its construction involves classism, racism, cronyism, patronage, politicking, and of course, unscrupulous real estate developers.

In 1851, the idea of a great park was proposed by Mayor Ambrose Kingsland, primarily because city aldermen recognized that the real estate holdings bordering Manhattan's seventeen public squares—which comprised a mere 165 acres—maintained the greatest value. Therefore, to encourage real estate development north of 42nd Street, a great park was needed. The initial plan detailed that a 150-acre park would be created from 66th to 75th streets, from Third Avenue to the East River. The strongest proponent of that plan was State Senator James William Beekman, the nephew of merchant James Beekman, who owned fifteen acres of land just one block south of the proposed park. Beekman

Squatter settlements and shantytowns were common in and around Central
     Park until about 1885

could profit mightily from increased real estate values, although he claimed that his primary interest was in enabling "all classes" of New Yorkers to share the "seaside breezes" of the waterfront. In typical New York fashion, dissent was prompt and passionate. Would "all" New Yorkers really benefit from an eastside park? Since most New Yorkers lived below 42nd Street, why was the park funded by general tax revenue, when it would only benefit uptown development?

The Special Committee on Parks recommended in 1852 that the park be constructed from 59th Street to 106th Street, from Fifth Avenue to Eighth Avenue. Recognizing the site's irregular topography—"numerous abrupt and rocky elevations, intersected constantly by ravines and gentle valleys"—made the place impractical for conventional real estate development. As a result, only a few parcels had ever been sold within this area; the state government owned much common land and would not need to purchase the property allocated for the reservoir. When compared with the numerous buy-outs they faced with the landowners of the East Side location, New Yorkers favored the lower per-acre acquisition cost. As it turned out, the aldermen who most virulently defended the site were also some of the first to speculate and profit by purchasing parcels of land adjacent to the proposed park, prior to its official designation.

Before development could begin, a design needed to be created, and the present landowners needed to move. Most of the people who owned land in the craggy marsh were African-Americans, it turned out (although in these years prior to the Civil War, black residents were not yet American voters). Back in 1825, Andrew Williams, a bootblack, bought three lots for $125 near 85th Street on the West side. His friend Epiphany Davis, a trustee on behalf of the African Methodist Episcopal Zion Church, bought twelve lots for $578, designating some of the land to build a church. More black families arrived, developing Seneca Village, a community of modest farms, also known as a safe haven for runaway slaves.

In 1853, park commissioners offered $700 per lot to each

Drive in Central Park under construction, 1860

landowner, a significant profit, but an end to a burgeoning community. On October 1, 1857, the residents of Seneca Village scattered, quietly and without violence, enabling the construction of Central Park. The African Methodist Episcopal Zion Church disappeared without a trace, although in 1959, a park gardener discovered a human skull, buried in what was once the graveyard of the church.

Meanwhile, a contest was announced: $2,000 would be paid to the designers of the best plan for a 1,778-acre park, with the costs not to exceed $1.5 million, about $34 million today. Furthermore, the park required four or more cross streets connecting Fifth to Eighth avenues, a twenty- to forty-acre parade ground for militia drills "with proper arrangements for the convenience of spectators," three playgrounds of up to ten acres each, a prominent fountain, a winter skating lake, and a lookout tower.

Thirty-three designs were submitted, with some courageous ideas: one suggested a massive fresco on the reservoir walls depicting the history of the American Revolution. Several proposals included an exhibition hall, concert hall, or lecture hall. Other proposals included: an open-air stadium for horse races; a one-third mile-long shooting gallery for cannons, muskets and pistols; bath houses for lake swimmers; a collection of Chinese, Norwegian, Italian, and Swiss lodges "to provide interest and variety;" and even a special lawn for women, equipped for gymnastics and archery, protected for privacy by a giant hedge. Some were concerned with issues beyond aesthetics: one called for mounted police and telegraph stations at every gate so that ruffians could be "marked, followed, watched, and annoyed in every way by

Frederick Law Olmsted, 1860

authorities;" another noted that the parade ground should be located away "from those parts on Eighth Avenue where drinking shops will be most likely to locate;" while another advocated that all carriages be banned, enabling New Yorkers of all economic backgrounds to appreciate the park as equals.

The winning entry was announced on April 28, 1858, awarding Calvert Vaux, an English architect, and Frederick Law Olmsted, the park superintendent, the opportunity to enact their vision. Above all, Olmsted and Vaux emphasized rural scenery, "to suggest the pleasant ideas of harmonious proportion, fitness, and agreeable variety to the eye." They also realized that carriages traveling through the park for recreation required different paths than those for "coal carts and butchers carts, dust carts and dung carts." By sinking the transverse roads eight feet beneath the park surface, commercial traffic would never jeopardize "those agreeable sentiments that we should wish the park to inspire." More than 100 years later, we still praise Olmsted and Vaux for their progressive thinking.

However, the park of today is not the park of Olmsted and

Vaux's vision. Almost from the day of its approval, commissioners tinkered with the design, often against the wishes of its designers. For starters, that $1.5 million allocation was woefully insufficient. To reduce costs, two transverse roads were eliminated, as were exterior iron fences, a music hall, and a conservatory. When Olmsted wrote that he was "thoroughly worn out, used up, fatigued beyond recovery," the commissioners advanced him $500 and sent him abroad for six weeks to "examine European parks," while work continued without his scrutiny. By the time of the park's completion in 1866, 20,000 laborers had moved nearly two and half million cubic yards of stone and earth. With hand tools and gunpowder they had broken through 300,000 cubic yards of gneiss rock veined with granite, stacked six million bricks, fertilized the land with 40,000 cubic yards of manure, and planted 270,000 trees and shrubs, for the then-exorbitant cost of $5 million (about $80 million today).

Even before it was finished, Central Park was welcomed with vigorous enthusiasm. To Olmsted and Vaux, that was the ultimate

The Grand Drive, Central Park, 1869

compliment. As aldermen predicted fifteen years earlier, the new park was a feat that befitted the greatness of the new city. With the stench of the swamp and farm animals a fuzzy memory, the properties flanking the park were now ripe for development. Even before the nine miles of carriage drives were completed, two-thirds of visitors arrived by carriage, confirming the upscale appeal of the properties surrounding the park. Sure enough, on the park's east side, the value of Fifth Avenue land tripled within only five years, as wealthy families built homes in a stretch soon designated as Millionaire's Row. When The Dakota was erected on the West Side, America's first luxury apartment house gave new meaning to "a room with a view"; it served as a model for future apartment houses that were erected on both sides of the park.

Today, no other city in the world can boast such an expanse of greenery at the foot of so many residences in the center of the city. The area's ever-escalating property values might be viewed as an unspoken tribute to the visions of Frederick Law Olmsted and Calvert Vaux.

❶ Central Park

② Proposed plan for Central Park
E. 66th to E. 75th sts. from
Third Ave. to the East River

③ Seneca Village
W. 82nd to W. 89th sts. between
Seventh and Eighth aves.

❹ The Dakota
One West 72nd St.

Key for Map

❶ Current location

⓪ Site no longer exists

CHAPTER 14

IT HAPPENED IN GRAMERCY PARK
THE COOPERATIVE GETS A LIFT

1832–1883

The first cooperative apartment house in New York was not on Fifth Avenue, it was at 34 Gramercy Park. The astounding story that precedes its inception reads like a mini-history of New York City, involving a lengthy list of celebrated New Yorkers.

Gramercy is an anglicized version of the Dutch word "crommessie," meaning "a small crooked knife," which referred to the shape of the brook that later flowed through giant conduits placed underground in the 1830s. The crommessie's wild terrain, dropping as much as forty feet in some areas, made farming impractical, but noting the city's booming population, landowner Samuel Ruggles raised a small fortune to move mountains of earth, divert water, and level the landscape to make it habitable. Today's New Yorkers pay plenty for a water view, but in the 1800s a brook simply meant mud, stench, and vermin—a definite detriment to residential development.

Ruggles had two radical ideas: to build townhouses around an open square, guaranteeing light and air, and to permit the owners

A crowd gathers around the home of former Governor Samuel J. Tilden, Gramercy Park, 1877

Samuel B. Ruggles

of those houses to maintain the parkland privately, free of government participation. That last idea was even more slippery than diverting the craggy brook, for New York City's government was loathe to give up the tax revenue from a potential block of houses. Yet Ruggles convinced the city's aldermen that residences facing a park would generate higher taxes than if they faced additional houses on the proposed park land. His argument worked. On February 13, 1832, the City decreed: ". . . the lands composing such square shall be exempted from taxation and assessment." To this day, Gramercy Park remains the only private park in Manhattan. Ruggles' grandson dedicated a monument to him within the park, a lasting tribute to the pioneer who made this unique oasis possible.

It took over a decade to landscape the oasis; meanwhile, Ruggles sold the surrounding lots to some of America's most powerful men, who retained great architects to plan their new homes. James Renwick, famed for his design of St. Patrick's Cathedral, designed the Calvary Church on the north side of the park. Calvert Vaux, co-designer of Central Park, built an opulent house at 15 Gramercy Park for Samuel Tilden, who lost the Presidential election in 1876 by one Electoral College vote. That carefully maintained manse is now the National Arts Club.

Other neighbors on or near the park soon included famed architect Stanford White, who redesigned many Gramercy Park interiors; Richard Morris Hunt, who later became known as the architect of the Metropolitan Museum; Cyrus Field, who laid the first transatlantic cable; inventor Peter Cooper, who earned a fortune on the B&O Railroad and later built Cooper Union; authors Edith Wharton, Herman Melville, Stephen Crane, Nathanael West and O. Henry; composers Victor Herbert and Antonín Dvořák; and the nineteenth century's most acclaimed actor, Edwin Booth. Along with Mark Twain and Stanford White, Booth formed the Players

Club, purchasing 16 Gramercy Park South in 1888 for $75,000, which White remodeled into a clubhouse. It was Booth's home for the final five years of his life, and remains one of Gramercy Park's highlights.

A few years earlier, in 1857, Elisha Graves Otis created a brilliant new gadget for hoisting heavy safes: he called his invention an elevator. His sons expanded it to accommodate passengers, then installed three elevators in 34 Gramercy Park South in 1883. With a tug on a rope within the elevator, water shifted between giant tanks in the basement and the rooftop, moving the elevator at fifty feet per minute as determined by the direction of the shifting water (a process still functioning within the building today, although the pump is no longer powered by steam). The result changed architecture, and Gramercy Park, forever.

The original building at 34 Gramercy had been a small hotel with stairs to each of its five stories. Demolished in 1880, new investors planned a taller hotel, with Louis Sherry's restaurant on the eighth floor. Before construction was completed, however, the

The view from 60 Gramercy Park North

investors opted not to proceed with the hotel, instead selling 6,500 shares in the building's corporation at $100 per share, allocated to units within the building. This historic action created the first cooperative apartment building in New York, an immediate sensation. Other co-ops soon followed; the concept of luxury apartment living soon displaced the charms of Gramercy Park's townhouses. More than half of them were demolished in the first half of the twentieth century to make room for luxury flats.

Within thirty years, New York boasted an estimated 40,000 apartment houses. A new era had begun.

❶ First co-op building
34 Gramercy Park South

❷ Calvary Church
277 Park Ave. South

❸ Samuel Tilden House
(National Arts Club)
15 Gramercy Park South

❹ The Players Club
16 Gramercy Park South

Street Scenes in Old New York

Cab stand at Madison Square, 1900

Clam seller in Mulberry Bend, c. 1900

Newsboys, 1910

Flatiron Building, 1902

On the streets in a New York blizzard, 1899

Tending a stand, Canal Street, 1910

A load of kimonos just finished,
Thompson Street, 1912

Miss Twombly and two ladies beside a coach, 1909

CHAPTER 15

THE GREAT WHITE WAY
THERE'S NO BUSINESS LIKE BROADWAY

1880–1930

New York is America's theater town. Mention "Broadway" to anyone in the world and they envision Times Square in Manhattan. For almost two *centuries* before professional sports arrived in America's largest city, New Yorkers flocked to attractions on a street called Broadway. "Show business" was born in New York.

The evolution of the American theater is closely linked to the growth of Manhattan. In the 1730s, when all New Yorkers lived downtown, Corbett's Tavern, near today's Bowling Green, featured a makeshift performance space, earning its reputation as New York's first theater. As new neighborhoods were constructed farther uptown, "concert saloons" became regular (though crude) fixtures throughout Manhattan. These rowdy establishments didn't just offer performers strutting their talents (viewed as one step above prostitution), they launched a new fad called "waiter-girls," barmaids who approached the patrons and plied them with liquor. Customers watched the show for as long as they kept buying drinks.

P. T. Barnum and General Tom Thumb

Other forms of entertainment arrived. One of the first entrepreneurs to reap a fortune on Broadway (at Ann Street) was P. T. Barnum, who displayed freaks for twenty-five cents per view (that's about seven dollars today). Between 1841 and 1865, when the entire population of the United States was thirty-two million, over thirty-eight million viewers paid to see Barnum's "mermaid" that was allegedly half fish and half monkey, plus a bearded lady, and a midget named General Tom Thumb. But for real entertainment in the 1800s, minstrel shows were the rage. A row of minstrel theaters soon stretched up Broadway from Grand Street to Houston Street, and then spilled over to the Bowery. Sparked perhaps by the Abolitionist movement in these pre-Civil War years, minstrels in blackface focused attention for the first time on the subculture of African Americans. Demand was so insatiable that P. T. Barnum added performers in blackface, and even Mayor Wood's brother opened a minstrel hall at 514 Broadway to cash in on the popularity.

Few traces of these theaters remain because they burned to the ground regularly. In the century leading up to Thomas Edison's life-changing lightbulb, theater footlights were open flames fueled by gas or oil. Then came limelight, a block of calcium that burned brightly when heated with hydrogen and oxygen. Limelights mounted on a balcony could illuminate the entire stage. Operators learned to focus it on a performer, much like today's spotlights (giving us the expression "in the limelight"). Theaters were flammable, but profitable enough to keep Broadway entrepreneurs rebuilding. Barnum's enterprise burned down twice. The second fire convinced the showman to try the circus instead.

In the 1850s, 14th Street was New York's most fashionable address, the neighborhood of prominent families. Following the notorious riot at the Astor Place Opera House in 1849, well-to-do neighbors invested $1000 per share to build a new opera house on 14th Street called the Academy of Music. With 4,000 seats on five levels, it was a monument to opera (and its investors), the world's largest opera house at the time. With more limelights than any theater in America, the Academy was also hailed for its acoustics half a century before the invention of amplified sound. To many in the audience, the intrigue over which prominent socialites would occupy the night's eighteen boxes held greater allure than the actual performance. Theaters became a place for America's aristocracy to mingle: men arrived in silk hats and formal attire; women wore gowns, jewels, and furs. The prospect of meeting an heiress during intermission was sufficient incentive for everyone to wear his or her finest, to participate in the club-like atmosphere. Theater was a communal experience to be savored shoulder-to-shoulder, not a personal one with waiter-girls and intoxicants (though they still proliferated). New York's elites assumed control of the theater. Their "Season" was rigidly observed, starting on September 1 (Labor Day wasn't invented until 1882) through June when the swells left sweltering Manhattan for cooler air in Newport, or Southampton or their camp in the Adirondacks. To this day, the Tony Awards observe this seasonal schedule.

The shareholders' business model was revolutionary. Their new opera house had no opera company. The Max Maretzek Italian Opera Company paid rent to present the first season (from October to December 1854), gambling on its

The Great Russian Ball at the Academy of Music, November 5, 1863

success at the box office. There was no arts-loving impresario at the Academy of Music; these were real estate deals transacted by a board of investors who sought the highest rent possible.

And that's show business. Entrepreneurs followed the money. More theaters cropped up around Broadway at Union Square, creating New York's first theater district. Adhering to the same seasonal schedule, their stock companies of actors and crew performed plays in rotation. As a building boom swept the city, show business grew into one of New York's biggest industries, with scenery shops, costume shops, play publishers, wig makers, agents, boarding houses, and hundreds of hopeful young actors moving in. Entrepreneurs soon realized: if the box office could break even on Broadway, then greater profits awaited when the production traveled by train to playhouses in other cities. Slick Broadway productions became a New York export.

A series of upheavals doomed the 14th Street theater district, sparking the Broadway of today. First, the city government passed the Concert Hall Act of 1862 in an effort to control public intoxication at concert saloons. The law required a $500 license from establishments that put on a show. No more free floorshow for as long as a drunkard kept buying booze. The hefty fee forced showplaces to issue tickets for scheduled performances, a major win for the upscale theaters on Broadway at Union Square.

The next blow hit hardest. As the box seats (with their associated social status) were passed down to another generation at the Academy of Music, the *nouveau riche* felt slighted. Roosevelts, Vanderbilts and robber barons demanded box seats and social prominence too. When the Academy burned down in 1866, it was promptly rebuilt with twenty-six boxes, but that was too meager an accommodation. These industrialists wanted a hand in the deal. In 1880, they joined forces and fortunes, announcing the creation of the Metropolitan Opera Association. Three years later, their new Metropolitan Opera House opened at distant 1411 Broadway, between 39th and 40th streets, surrounded by livery stables and carriage builders. The immediate acclaim for the opera house soon sent those businesses packing. Not only was the Metropolitan Opera larger and more elaborate than the Academy of Music, featuring three tiers of boxes to showcase the wealth of every economic leader in Manhattan, its impresario actually developed a resident company. The Met soon produced its own operas, and, starting in 1884, it went on tour just like Broadway shows. (First provincial stop? Brooklyn.) Back on fading 14th Street, the Academy of Music canceled its 1886 opera season and switched to vaudeville. Old-timers mourned when the Academy of Music was demolished in 1926 (to become today's Con Edison Building at the corner of Irving Place.)

Then came the perfect storm: In 1882, Edison invented the lightbulb, inspiring unfathomed possibilities for the stage and the streets. In 1893, Charles Frohman opened what could be credited as the first "Broadway lights:" the electrified Empire Theatre at 1430

Notable Broadway theaters (clockwise from top left): Casino Theatre at 39th Street and Broadway (1882-1930); New York Theatre at 44th Street and Broadway (former Olympia Theatre, 1895-1935); The Hippodrome at 43rd Street and Sixth Avenue (1905-1939); Shubert Theatre at 225 West 44th Street (1913-)

Broadway, across from the Metropolitan Opera House, the next link toward establishing a theater district. A short distance to the north stood Longacre Square, where Broadway and Seventh Avenue crossed in a long, broad expanse, notable for its wide swath of sky. Oscar Hammerstein was the first to build there; his massive Olympia Theatre stretched along Broadway from 44th to 45th Streets. In 1902, publisher Arthur Ochs bought the triangular wedge of property at the center of Longacre Square where he built a twenty-five-story tower for his newspaper, the *New York Times*. It was the second tallest building in Manhattan. Then the first subway opened under the Times Building in October 1904. Hammerstein promptly built three more theaters, and today's Broadway was born. City aldermen renamed the place Times Square. With electric lights illuminating every marquee, Broadway became known as the Great White Way.

For the next three decades, the vicinity was a constant construction site, reaching its peak in 1928, when seventy-one legitimate theaters presented 257 productions in one season. Many lessons were learned along the way. Americans discovered "dining out." Fashionable restaurants moved in, and hotels too, all competing against movie moguls for space in Times Square. Antiquated stock companies were disbanded because entrepreneurs learned from the Academy of Music: theater owners don't need to be the show's producers too. It's a real estate deal. With a top ticket price of $6.60, owning a theater was more lucrative than owning an apartment

Times Square, 1920s

house. It didn't matter if the shows were hits or flops. Just collect the rent. The economics were straightforward: It cost nearly $1 million to construct a theater during those boom years. A hit show could gross more than that in a year, from which

In the musical *Annie Get Your Gun* in 1946, Ethel Merman and cast introduced what became her signature song "There's No Business Like Show Business"

the theater owner collected forty percent of the gross receipts as rent. From that $400,000 the owner paid overhead expenses, but all of the show's production costs were borne by the producer. It was practically impossible for theater owners not to make money. They could pocket substantial profits within just a few years. Three young brothers named Shubert bought into that concept in a big way, building theaters in the Times Square area and more across the country. They did the math: Producers paid to develop new shows on Broadway. Then, when a show exhausted its audience in New York, the producer could stretch two more years of pure profit from the show by transporting its scenery, costumes, and actors to new audiences elsewhere. The Shuberts and their rivals constructed palatial theaters in downtowns across America, providing the venues for shows that arrived "direct from Broadway."

On December 31, 1907, when electric lights sparkled in Times Square, the *New York Times* instituted an annual event: lowering an electrically lighted ball down the tower's seventy-foot flagpole at midnight to proclaim the arrival of another year. That ball has dropped for more than 100 years now, with no end in sight. The same can be said for its neighbors. Times Square is the most visited place on the globe annually; Broadway grosses and attendance at its long-running shows continue to break records. Forty legitimate theaters, now protected landmarks, offer something to delight everyone. From classics and revivals, to hip-hop musicals, jukebox musicals, dramas, comedies, and one-man or one-woman shows, there's something for everyone on Broadway today. The most intoxicating melting pot, live theater is still a communal experience to be savored shoulder-to-shoulder in New York.

Show Talk

"Step into the limelight" isn't the only showbiz expression to find its way into vernacular use. Consider these words and phrases that are rooted in the theater:

Hypocrite–from the ancient Greek *hypokrites*, was a reference to actors, because they pretend to be someone they are not, and they express scripted beliefs or feelings that are not necessarily their own. Today, hypocrisy is not limited to actors!

Claptrap–a cheap shot that always gets applause. Early in the twentieth century, for example, composer George M. Cohan wrote patriotic musicals that ended with huge ovations just by waving a flag onstage. Today, *Webster's* defines claptrap as: "showy, insincere talk intended only to get applause." Politicians, take note!

It ain't over till the fat lady sings–A not-so-kind reference to an opera diva's final aria, the big song near the end of the performance before she stabs her lover, or jumps to her death, or other dramatic twists that lead to the show's conclusion. Also known as the . . .

Eleven o'clock number–Back when the elites ran Broadway, shows started after dinner, at 8:30 p.m. and ran for exactly two and a half hours. The big production number that closed the show or resolved the plot landed at 11 p.m. Now it means the big finish to any kind of project, and on Broadway, the eleven o'clock number almost *never* arrives at 11 p.m. anymore.

Break a leg–A leg is the curtain or proscenium on the left and right sides of the stage. In vaudeville, when more individual acts were hired than could fit on the bill, only the acts that broke past the legs to be seen by the audience got paid. Since it's bad luck to say "Good Luck" to anyone inside a theater (*"With all this natural talent, why would I need luck?"*), wishing that an actor break past the legs to get paid is the kindest compliment of all.

① Academy of Music

② Casino Theatre
1404 Broadway

③ Metropolitan Opera House
1411 Broadway

④ Empire Theatre
1430 Broadway

⑤ Olympia Theatre
1514-1516 Broadway

❻ The New York Times Tower
1475 Broadway (One Times Square)

⑦ The Hippodrome
1120 Ave. of the Americas

❽ Shubert Theatre
225 West 44th St.

CHAPTER 16

ASSASSINATION OF AN ARCHITECT
THE STORY OF STANFORD WHITE

1906

The "trial of the century" and the scandalous demise of New York's foremost *fin-de-siècle* architect, Stanford White, is gleefully detailed in E. L. Doctorow's 1975 novel and the Broadway musical *Ragtime*. White's accomplishments while living merit a few songs too, for no Gilded Age designer succeeded better at charming New York's aristocrats, living in a style more ebullient than fiction, then leaving behind the architectural legacy that defines an era.

As the son of a journalist and theater reviewer, young Stanford took celebrity for granted at an early age. His father's friend Frederick Law Olmsted, the famed designer of Central Park, delivered sixteen-year-old Stanny to an architect, for whom he apprenticed shortly after the Civil War. The diversity of White's knowledge is astounding to modern professionals, for his grasp of clients' needs, command of exterior construction, and remarkable application of interior details displays pure genius. He engineered building foundations that few would ever see, envisioned the

exteriors that all might admire, then determined every decorative nuance, designing elements in stone, woodwork, glass, plaster, metals, and ceramics. Overseeing his project from concept to completion made Stanford White the darling of New York's gentry, as the city abounded with new construction. In 1879 he joined Charles McKim and William Rutherford Mead in forging the firm of McKim, Mead & White.

One of White's first projects was a splendid mansion on East 72nd Street for the famed jeweler Charles L. Tiffany, including a top floor apartment and massive studio for the jeweler's son Louis, who would soon gain fame as a decorative stained-glass artisan. From that day on, impressive commissions never ceased, including Judson Memorial Church at 55 Washington Square South, the Washington Square Arch, and his crowning achievement, the second Madison Square Garden at 26th Street and Madison Avenue.

Amid these impressive assignments, White lived beyond his means, collecting art, investing in shows, entertaining lavishly, often in the apartment he maintained atop Madison Square Garden. At age fifty, with his son studying architecture at Harvard while his wife occupied their elegant townhouse at 121 East 21st Street, Stanford began a scandalous affair with Evelyn Nesbit, a sixteen-year-old chorus girl appearing on Broadway in *Floradora*.

Two years later, Evelyn dumped him for actor John Barrymore, then married millionaire cocaine addict Harry K. Thaw, heir to a railroad fortune. Soon after the marriage, upon learning that his wife's virginity had been lost years earlier to White, the enraged

Harry K. Thaw and Stanford White

Stanford White's masterpiece, Madison Square Garden, 1901

Thaw hired four private investigators to trail White.

On June 25, 1906, White attended the opening night of *Mam'zelle Champagne*, a revue in which he invested, at the Madison Square Garden roof garden theater. In the middle of a number called "I Could Love a Million Girls," Thaw shot him three times at point blank range. White died instantly, and was buried on Long Island. Newspapers everywhere printed lurid details of the scandal for months.

Thaw was tried, declared not guilty by reason of insanity, and spent seven years in an asylum. Promptly upon his return to society, he divorced Evelyn. She returned to the stage, took drugs, attempted suicide, sold her story to the movies (she's played by youthful Joan Collins in *The Girl In The Red Velvet Swing*), and died in 1967 at age eighty-two.

Despite his grand lifestyle, Stanford White died approximately $500,000 in debt. In four auctions, his treasures were sold. William Randolph Hearst bought his dining room ceiling for $3,000. The Metropolitan Museum acquired the baroque doorway from White's picture gallery. His wife retired to a modest Long Island cottage, and auctioned their remaining furniture to survive the Depression.

① Tiffany Mansion
East 72nd St. at Madison Ave.

❷ Judson Memorial Church
55 Washington Sq. South

❸ Washington Square Arch
Fifth Ave. at Washington Sq.

④ Madison Square Garden (1890)
Madison Ave. at E. 26th St.

⑤ White Townhouse
121 East 21st St.

❻ Villard Mansion
Madison Ave. at E. 50th St.

❼ The Metropolitan Club
1 East 60th St.

❽ The Harmonie Club
4 East 60th St.

❾ The Players Club
16 Gramercy Park South

⑩ Colony Club (American Academy of Dramatic Arts): 120 Madison Ave.

⑪ 972 Fifth Ave.
(French Embassy)

⑫ Herald Building
Broadway at 34th St.

⑬ Sherry's Hotel
Fifth Ave. at 44th St.

⑭ The Original Penn Station
Eighth Ave. between W. 31st and W. 33rd sts

Stanford White's New York

Even better than the delightful songs in *Ragtime*, the happiest memories of Stanford White's prolific career can be celebrated throughout New York City. Though altered over time, his projects document an opulent Manhattan lifestyle that can no longer be replicated, including: the Villard Mansion on Madison Avenue at 50th Street (now New York Palace), The Metropolitan Club (1 East 60th Street), the Harmonie Club (4 East 60th Street), The Players Club (16 Gramercy Park), the original Colony Club (120 Madison Avenue), 972 Fifth Avenue (now the French Embassy); the list goes on.

Among the "lost" buildings are: the second Madison Square Garden, the Herald Building (headquarters for the *New York Herald*), Sherry's Hotel (and its famous ice cream parlor at Fifth Avenue at 44th Street), and the glorious Penn Station (occupied by contemporary Madison Square Garden), which was completed after White's death.

From top: The Colony Club, the Villard Mansion, and Penn Station

CHAPTER 17

ART IN AN ALLEY
THE ASHCAN SCHOOL AND THE CARRIAGE HOUSES OF GREENWICH VILLAGE

1840–1950

Stories abound about life in the magnificent brick townhouses along the northern edge of Washington Square, home to some of New York's most influential characters. The *untold* story is of the cobblestone alleys *behind* the elegant row, where socialites parked their horses and carriages.

In those days, New Yorkers traveled in horse-drawn carriages much the way we ride buses today, following specific routes and schedules. Only aristocrats could afford their own carriages and horses, along with the requisite housing that kept both safe from the elements. The carriage and the team, and sometimes even the stable boy, lived in a low-rise building near the family's townhouse. They weren't especially beautiful, but they were extremely practical, with high ceilings and wide doorframes through which to navigate the carriage, plus a loft or two above for hay and storage.

Today, carriage houses remain scattered throughout the boroughs; the most notable ones are clustered in areas like Sniffen

Court in Murray Hill, and in two beautiful cobblestone alleys in Greenwich Village: Washington Mews, accessible from Fifth Avenue and University Place, and MacDougal Alley, accessible from MacDougal Street just south of 8th Street.

Around the corner from the Washington Mews and those notable townhouses, John William Draper took his sister onto the roof of the science department at New York University in 1840. He snapped her picture with a primitive camera—this was the first image of a human face in sunlight. With the emergence of the camera, photographers like Jacob Riis and Matthew Brady, with his gut-wrenching photographs of Civil War battles, documented the realities of the moment.

As photographers began to chronicle the matter-of-fact, artists were left to dream and disturb convention in what they called "the new realism." Rejecting the short, precise brush strokes of masters like Rembrandt, new artists defied reality and famously established Greenwich Village as America's primary art colony.

In 1858, Richard Morris Hunt designed the Tenth Street Studio Building, just east of Sixth Avenue, the country's first centralized facility for artists. It provided light, privacy, and showrooms for its twenty-five residents, enabling painters and sculptors to live and work in single spacious studios, and thus, the "studio apartment" was born. The artists who embraced this radical lifestyle became some of the most revered names in American art: Winslow Homer, William Merritt Chase, and John La Farge; their works hang in major museums today. An instant success, the Tenth Street Studios soon lured influential critics, affluent patrons, and the curious public to its well-publicized "visiting days."

Other factors influenced the art scene. As New York's population exploded, the city's boundaries pushed northward, where snazzy buildings grew taller and taller. Greenwich Village, by contrast, looked dilapidated. The wealthy families of Washington Square had headed to fashionable surroundings uptown, relinquishing Greenwich Village to those who sought lower rents. Many townhouses were carved into tiny flats and rooming houses,

The Tenth Street Studio by William Merritt Chase, 1880

and these became dense havens for writers, performers, musicians, and artists. Low-rise architecture guaranteed good sunlight for the artists and the rent was cheap. (As late as 1934, a four-room apartment on Grove Street was only $20 a month; that's about $350 today.)

Synergy among the bohemians was inevitable. As artists showcased their creations, Village writers trumpeted the news: Greenwich Village was the most inspired source of art in America. Across the street from the Tenth Street Studios, a collection of artists, including Stanford White and Augustus Saint-Gaudens, formed the Tile Club, reveling in the Village's creative energies.

Within adjacent blocks, the greatest American painters established their studios: John Singer Sargent, Grant Wood, George Bellows, Edward Hopper, the list continues impressively. And photography wasn't far behind. Matthew Brady opened a gallery nearby to display his Civil War photos. With no wealthy neighbors seeking shelter for their horses, the Village carriage houses were

Gertrude Vanderbilt Whitney poses for the January 1917 issue of *Vogue* magazine

almost forgotten. Then came Gertrude Vanderbilt Whitney.

In 1907, the enormously wealthy Whitney planned a career as a sculptor, which required a workspace with a high ceiling. She struck up friendships with local artists, and rented 19 MacDougal Alley.

The carriage house made a perfect studio: sunlight streamed through its high, wide doorframe, while the ceiling height guaranteed the creative space every sculptor needs. Mrs. Whitney soon became a patron to several artists working in or near the carriage houses; in 1914, their first group show in the remodeled MacDougal Alley studio caused an uproar.

Critics and patrons accustomed to plush surroundings sneered at art displayed in an alley, especially since it audaciously depicted the grimier details of life. The artists were dubbed the Ashcan School, a distinction they wore with pride. Artist Robert Henri was an admirer of the down-to-earth realism of artists like Thomas Eakins; other Ashcan artists included George Bellows, William Glackens, George Luks, Everett Shinn, and John Sloan. Mrs. Whitney bought four of their paintings and a building at 8 West 8th Street to display them. The Whitney Museum of American Art was born.

For the first half of the twentieth century, some of the greatest names in modern art—Mark Rothko, Barnett Newman, Jackson Pollock, and Robert Motherwell—thrived on the bohemian energy of Greenwich Village. The Ashcan artists eventually moved on to greater fame and larger spaces, while the carriage houses were transformed into homes. Their great doorframes were sealed to become picture windows, plumbing and heat were installed, and soon the former stables were small but valuable homes in quaint Village cul-de-sacs. Today, the Washington Mews carriage houses are part of New York University. A new Whitney Museum was erected at the entrance to the High Line on Gansevoort Street.

❶ Sniffen Court

❷ Washington Mews

❸ MacDougal Alley

④ Tenth Street Studio
   51 West 10th St.

⑤ Tile Club
   58 West 10th St.

❻ Gertrude Whitney's Gallery
   8 West 8th St.

McSorley's Bar, John Sloan, 1912, Detroit Institute of Arts

New York Scenes by Ashcan School Artists

Snow in New York, Robert Henri, 1902,
National Gallery of Art

Central Park, Winter, William Glackens, c. 1905,
The Metropolitan Museum of Art

The Haymarket, Sixth Avenue, John Sloan, 1907,
Brooklyn Museum

Six O'clock, Winter, John Sloan, 1912,
The Phillips Collection

*The Orchestra Pit: Old Proctor's Fifth
Avenue Theatre*, Everett Shinn, 1906,
Yale University Art Gallery

Street Scene (Hester Street), George Luks, 1905, Brooklyn Museum

CHAPTER 18

APARTMENT LIFE
THE DAKOTA AND THE GOLDEN AGE
1884–1929

Once upon a time in New York, anyone who was anyone resided in a townhouse, while aspiring to own a Fifth Avenue mansion. Yet, with the advent of apartment living at The Dakota in 1884, New Yorkers abandoned their brownstone stoops to head for the elevators.

Townhouses offered cross-ventilation, ample rooms for children and storage, special entrances for servants, backyards for beating the carpets. Why would anyone forego these urban conveniences to live anonymously, stacked beneath other similarly miserable denizens? Undesirable, multiple-unit buildings flourished in many squalid pockets across the city. Those noisy, drafty, and unsafe tenements housed the immigrant peasants who arrived in staggering multitudes daily at Ellis Island to work in sweatshops. Every resident in a tenement flat dreamed of escaping such squalor. Who would choose to live like them?

But New Yorkers knew other facts about those apartment flats. Unlike the best townhouses on Washington Square, tenements

Edward Clark

had real indoor plumbing; no outhouses, no cisterns, no chamber pots. It was not uncommon for a servant to labor all day in a high-profile townhouse, only to return to more modern amenities in an apartment. Soon, Edward Clark, co-owner of the Singer Sewing Machine Company, recognized several oncoming trends and devised a radical scheme.

Clark saw that New York was a boomtown. Business was great, thanks to the steady supply of cheap European labor. And, thanks to the Industrial Revolution, businesses were expanding exponentially; as more companies opened, more employees were flocking to New York. Housing just couldn't keep pace with demand, one reason why tenements were so grossly overpopulated. Yet Clark knew that in European cities, the gentry had been living in elegant flats for decades. Surmising that the resistance to apartment life in America stemmed solely from the negative associations New Yorkers made as they observed the discomforts of tenement dwellers, Clark seized the opportunity to erect a building that could never be confused with a tenement.

Dubbed "Clark's Folly" while it was being constructed, The Dakota earned its name by being located so far beyond metropolitan New York that visitors exclaimed that they were traveling to Dakota Territory. Clark knew his building's success would stem from his marketing acumen. By word of mouth alone, he sold the amenities as strongly as the apartments themselves. The Dakota offered two top floors of servants' rooms for the staff of the primary residents below, while the second floor was designed as a collection of hotel-style suites for tenants to house their visiting guests. Since a carriage ride in 1884 from Washington Square to The Dakota required half a day, dark approached by the time a guest completed a social call at The Dakota. Fearing nighttime assaults by Eighth Avenue "highwaymen," an overnight stay in The Dakota became a welcomed ritual. After all, it was the only apartment house in America with four passenger elevators. It also boasted over 200 miles of plumbing.

View north from the roof of The Dakota, 1887

The overnight guestrooms were a stroke of marketing genius. As visitors became more comfortable with The Dakota's location and the new Central Park, the viability of an entire neighborhood was born. Still unfinished when the building first opened, Clark installed a mini-Con Edison underground in the adjacent lot, with furnaces massive enough to provide steam not just to The Dakota, but to "all the blocks from the north side of 70th Street to the south side of 74th Street between Eighth and Columbus Avenues" along with generators for "electric illumination." (There was no electricity above Spruce Street in 1884.) For those traditionalists who preferred fireplaces—Clark's apartment had seventeen—the building's staff provided firewood and coal, and ashes were swept out daily.

Unlike the low ceilings of most townhouses (where high ceilings just meant more stairs to climb), life in a "French flat," as Dakota architect Henry Hardenbergh put it, provided rooms on a grand scale. Apartments on low floors at The Dakota had fifteen-foot ceilings, while servants' quarters featured twelve-foot ceiling heights, and just about every apartment had a drawing room, some the size of ballrooms.

Upon the building's completion on October 27, 1884, the *New York Graphic* published a 2,500-word article that called The Dakota "the most perfect apartment house in the world." The story gushed that The Dakota "guaranteed to the tenants comforts which would require unlimited wealth in a private residence." It was the endorsement Clark longed to hear, for it confirmed the viability of luxury apartments, the first in the Western Hemisphere. But sadly, unbeknownst to many tenants, Clark died almost two years before the building's completion. He left the entire ownership of The Dakota to his grandson, who was also his namesake. When the building opened and the money flooded in, tenants wrote their monthly rent checks to their landlord Edward S. Clark, a twelve-year-old boy.

Following the *New York Graphic* story, which was reprinted in the *New York Times*, downtowners thronged to the city's newest attraction with hundreds of requests for apartments, but it was too late. Without a single advertisement, The Dakota was fully rented; a ten-room apartment went for $3,000 per year (about $78,000 today). Townhouses were abruptly passé; the Age of the Apartment House had arrived. Once again, construction could not keep pace with demand.

Now architects and builders faced a new problem. How quickly could they meet the demands of consumers who suddenly wished to live in luxury flats? Who even knew how to design or build one of those newfangled "skyscrapers?" Into this uncertain environment came Emery Roth, one of the most prolific but uncelebrated

architects in New York history. With luck, good timing, and spectacular craftsmanship, Emery Roth permanently changed the New York City skyline, designing the most magnificent residences the city had ever seen.

Emery Roth was a Hungarian-Jewish immigrant with no

formal training. He apprenticed to the architects that built the World's Columbian Exposition in Chicago in 1893, then came to New York, where Richard Morris Hunt's firm paid him $25 per week to sketch private residences. He also studied the Stuyvesant Apartments built by Hunt on East 18th Street, where "luxury flats" accessed by elevators had private indoor plumbing, unlike the squalid tenements nearby.

Park Avenue at 61st Street, 1924

In 1899, Roth secured his first major commission: the Saxony Apartments on Broadway and 82nd Street, followed soon after by the Hotel Belleclaire on Broadway at 77th Street, the first residential structure in Manhattan to be entirely supported by a steel frame.

As the Hotel Belleclaire was rising above Broadway, Leo and Alexander Bing arrived at Roth's office; they were brothers who sold plots of land to speculative builders, then provided the building loans. Observing his knowledge of modern high-rise architecture, the brothers proposed that Roth oversee their upcoming projects, a relationship that stretched over three decades, as Roth designed forty-five buildings for Bing & Bing, from Greenwich Village to Washington Heights.

Meanwhile, New York was in turmoil. Between 1899 and 1913, the assessed value of Manhattan real estate increased by 207 percent. The soaring taxes sent even well-to-do families out of their single-family homes. Apartments were the new option. Even millionaires lived in them. A flat could have more rooms than a brownstone, all on one floor, plus servants' quarters and running water in multiple baths.

When the trains in the tunnel under Park Avenue were

electrified in 1905, the noise and soot subsided. Park Avenue became the grand new boulevard where Roth could develop large plots of land into high-rise apartment houses. His first Park Avenue construction was the graceful 570 Park, built of white marble and red brick, decorated with white terra cotta. He designed the facade of 417 Park, constructed entirely of limestone. At 1000 Park Avenue, he designed a massive building of brown brick. The two gothic figures that flank the main entrance, one a warrior and the other a builder, are rumored to be modeled after his clients Leo and Alexander Bing.

Following World War I, America's consumer purchasing power increased dramatically. The pent-up demand for housing stimulated an enormous construction boom, especially in New York. From 1920 to 1930, New York City accounted for twenty percent of all residential construction in the entire nation. Back in 1919, apartment buildings accounted for only about thirty-nine percent of new construction; by 1926, that figure was seventy-seven percent. With hotels included, high-rise residential buildings accounted for eighty-five percent of all construction in New York City between 1927 and 1930. Townhouses were history.

This was an era of great prosperity, and the golden age of apartment house construction; Emery Roth's skills were in high demand all over town. He designed majestic focal points such as 480 Park Avenue, along with less prominent "background buildings" including 221 West 82nd Street and 228 West 83rd Street. For Bing & Bing he created 39 Fifth Avenue, 10 Sheridan Square, and 310 West End Avenue. Controversy arose when Bing & Bing constructed Roth's design for the Hotel Dorset at 30 West 54th Street, a large building on the same narrow block as the hallowed mansion of John D. Rockefeller, Jr. To escape the invasion of businesses and apartment houses, the Rockefellers moved away.

Roth continued to develop hotels, designing The Drake at 440 Park Avenue and The Alden at 222 Central Park West, his eventual home after his children had grown. Along Fifth Avenue, he designed 1115, 1125, 1133, and 1200, as well as 784, 1009, 1112, and 1175 Park Avenue.

Central Park with the San Remo in the background, 1942

To encourage new construction, New York City redefined its zoning laws, permitting high-rises where modest five-story dwellings once stood. The new zoning laws were put to the test when Emery Roth was retained to create the Ritz Tower at Park Avenue and 57th Street in 1926. Unlike the fifteen-story buildings he frequently called his "skyscratchers," the Ritz reached a soaring forty-one stories, dominating the Manhattan skyline, a true residential skyscraper. From the top of the completed building, an unbroken view opened for twenty-five miles in every direction, which Roth proclaimed to be "a panorama unexcelled in all New York." Although at least one critic referred to it as a "skypuncture," New Yorkers understood the need for this new generation of slender, stepped-back towers of unprecedented heights.

Roth planned opulence in every corner of the Ritz Tower, from grand entertaining rooms on the ground floor, profuse ornamentation inside and out, to a new kind of cooperative arrangement for maids and valets. Instead of providing servants' quarters within individual units, the Ritz Tower provided a staff for all tenants. Servants wages were included in the rent, an appealing amenity to wealthy tenants seeking to reduce their daily expenses without compromising their lifestyles. At the opening banquet on November 15, 1926, Mayor Jimmy Walker and other distinguished New Yorkers unanimously praised the labors of Emery Roth, the

Fifth Avenue and the Grand Army Plaza, north
toward Central Park, 1910-1930

self-taught immigrant
whose work represented
the cutting edge of
ingenuity.

Roth was soon
awarded his two most
important commissions:
The Beresford and the
San Remo on Central
Park West. Situated
at a corner where two
parks—Central Park
and Manhattan Square,
home to the American
Museum of Natural
History—meet, The
Beresford rises twenty-
two stories and from a
distance resembles an
impregnable fortress;
upon closer inspection
it blends harmoniously into its site.

Similar luxury was built into the San Remo to far more startling
effect. Studying the new zoning laws, Roth understood that
residential buildings could achieve new heights if setbacks and
courtyards were provided in exchange. He devised the first twin-
towered skyscraper, adding two eleven-story towers above the San
Remo's seventeen-story base. The ingenious concept completely
eliminated the need for hallways, since each tower floor was
occupied by one private apartment, with light and air from every
direction, along with views as glorious as those at the Ritz.

Then the bubble burst. As the stock market crashed in 1929,
the San Remo failed to lure wealthy tenants. One year after its
construction, thirty percent of the apartments remained vacant. In
Central Park, directly across from the San Remo's sparkling lobby,

penniless people built shanties of tin and tarpaper. The bank that held the San Remo's mortgage collapsed just months after the building opened; its officers were indicted for speculating with depositors' funds. After a series of bankruptcies and rent rollbacks, the largest apartments were subdivided. Every two-story apartment in the south tower was cut into two single-floor units. The Beresford suffered a similar fate. In 1940, the San Remo and The Beresford were sold together for $25,000 cash over the existing mortgages. In 1929, the buildings had been valued at approximately $10 million. The golden age of apartment construction was over. No one, not even Emery Roth, erected buildings like those ever again.

Just as America entered World War II, Roth was commissioned to build 875 Fifth Avenue, (possibly the last building any broker can call "prewar"). To erect the building, three grand mansions were to be razed, including one designed by Roth's mentor, Richard M. Hunt. When the war ended, Roth was retained to build a cooperative at 880 Fifth Avenue, across the street from his recent project. Displaying the plans to his son Richard, who had just returned home from the Navy, the younger Roth's suggestions for revisions were so extensive that the father recognized that this was the project to pass to his son. At the corner of Fifth Avenue and 69th Street, Emery Roth's final building, 875 Fifth Avenue, stands on the foundation of his mentor, facing the first project developed by his son: 880 Fifth Avenue. The firm of Emery Roth & Sons was established months later.

The Dakota and New York Residences by Emery Roth & Sons

San Remo

10 Sheridan Square

Ritz Tower

417 Park Avenue

The Beresford

480 Park Avenue

39 Fifth Avenue

880 Fifth Avenue

875 Fifth Avenue

1. The Dakota
2. Saxony Apartments
3. Hotel Belleclaire
4. 570 Park Ave.
5. 417 Park Ave.
6. 1000 Park Ave.
7. 480 Park Ave.
8. 221 West 82nd St.
9. 228 West 83rd St.
10. 39 Fifth Ave.
11. 10 Sheridan Sq.
12. 310 West End Ave.
13. Hotel Dorset
14. The Drake
15. The Alden
16. 1115 Fifth Ave.
17. 1125 Fifth Ave.
18. 1133 Fifth Ave.
19. 1200 Fifth Ave.
20. 784 Park Ave.
21. 1009 Park Ave.
22. 1112 Park Ave.
23. 1175 Park Ave.
24. Ritz Tower
25. The Beresford
26. San Remo
27. 875 Fifth Ave.
28. 880 Fifth Ave.

CHAPTER 19

LOWER EAST SIDE
AN IMMIGRANT TALE

1900–

In 1900, it was tough to be a Jew in Europe. Russian pogroms pushed people from their homes, dividing families through needless violence and intolerance. Other nations forced other indignities, leading many Jews to give up their homes in Europe to pursue new lives elsewhere. For many, Ellis Island in New York Harbor was the first stop.

Great waves of Jewish immigrants arrived in Manhattan during the first decades of the twentieth century. Although they came from Russia, Prussia, Austria-Hungary, Lithuania and many other nations, these immigrants found unity through the Yiddish language they all shared. They settled into the tenements to the east of Little Italy in the Lower East Side, a neighborhood that stretches from Canal Street up to Houston Street, from the Bowery to the East River.

By 1915, 320,000 Jews lived on the Lower East Side, making it one of the most densely populated places in America. Most tenements were constructed with four apartments per floor, with

The Cottone family works together finishing garments in a tenement, hoping to make two dollars a week, 1913

bathtubs in the kitchens and communal toilets out in the hall. In the humid New York summer, the fire escape provided a place to sleep, away from the tenement's stale air. The neighborhood became known for its ethnic cuisine, places like Katz's Deli and Yonah Schimmel Knish Bakery became local institutions that serve traditional food to this day.

Not everyone was Jewish. Italians, Poles, and other Eastern-Europeans joined in the mix, united in their poverty as well as in their aspirations for a bright new start in America. In the early twentieth century, jobs were controlled by ethnicities in matter-of-fact New York. Irishmen were cops, the Chinese ran the laundries, Germans owned the breweries; soon the residents of the Lower East Side became famous for developing New York's garment industry into a national powerhouse. The sweatshops along Broadway were packed with laborers from the Lower East Side: pieceworkers who were paid by the number of sleeves or zippers or pockets they sewed. Tailors who owned their own sewing machines frequently strapped

Lower East Side eviction, 1910

those machines to their backs, then took extra work home each night. The garment industry moved uptown (and around the world).

In the past twenty years, the neighborhood has undergone one of the most remarkable transformations the city has ever seen. Once a symbol of urban blight, today the Lower East Side is gentrified almost beyond recognition. The artists arrived first, followed by luxury developers during the boom years of the early twenty-first century. Now, the aging tenements stand beside luxurious apartment houses in this ever-evolving neighborhood, along with upscale markets, trendy cafés, hip nightspots and the shimmering New Museum of Contemporary Art. Today's Lower East Side offers something for everyone.

1 Katz's Deli
205 East Houston St.

2 Yonah Schimmel Knish Bakery
137 East Houston St.

3 New Museum
235 Bowery

4 Lower East Side Tenement Museum
103 Orchard St.

THE LOWER EAST SIDE TODAY

Discover the area's rich history at the Lower East Side Tenement Museum, located at 103 Orchard Street, which offers guided tours of an adjacent restored nineteenth-century tenement at 97 Orchard Street. Built in 1863, the building was home to more than 7,000 working-class immigrants. The home, uninhabited for fifty years before it was restored, was like a time capsule, and now contains six restored apartments.

After your tour, taste the neighborhood's history at Katz's Deli or Yonah Schimmel Knish Bakery on nearby Houston Street.

CHAPTER 20

PROHIBITION AND ALL THAT JAZZ
THE SPEAKEASY DAYS OF NEW YORK CITY

1920–1932

Good times abounded in 1918 when World War I ended. New Yorkers embraced bold new lifestyles; wealthy families gave up their costly mansions for modern apartments in Park Avenue "skyscrapers." Gone were formal dinners of grand cuisine: "cocktail parties" were all the rage. Women gained the right to vote, then promptly cut their hair and hemlines, exposing calves for the first time in a millennium. Couples who once waltzed at arms length now tangoed cheek-to-cheek, while "flappers" danced the Charleston to the newfangled rhythm called jazz.

It was too good to remain unchallenged. When a Minnesota Congressman introduced an Amendment to the U.S. Constitution that made alcoholic beverages illegal, America faced a political cataclysm. In a puritanical tantrum, the House and Senate overrode President Wilson's veto, making Prohibition a federal law on January 16, 1920. The nation's new wave of morality crashed hard

against New York's good time revolution. Manhattan real estate was soon put to some surprising new uses.

"No liquor?!" The federal government padlocked about 16,000 barrooms in New York, while the highest-profile restaurants in New York closed rather than serve meals without champagne or cocktails. Famous institutions like Delmonico's were shuttered, while Louis Sherry turned his celebrated cafe into an ice cream parlor. One French restaurant clung to business by mixing water or seltzer into its wines, reducing the alcohol level to an acceptable three percent, but New Yorkers weren't buying it. Instead, they supported a far more clandestine industry: illegal "speakeasies" where hard liquor came with assorted adventures. New York soon had an estimated 32,000 speakeasies as Prohibition ratcheted up the excitement of living in the Jazz Age.

The first place for speakeasies to proliferate was, predictably, in Greenwich Village. New York's bohemia was the ideal spot for celebrating the civil liberties society attempted to deny, and

Speakeasy by Henry Patrick Raleigh, 1925

drinking became an act of defying authority. Through the Village's maze of winding side streets, walk-up apartments turned into distribution centers for homemade spirits. Village "tea rooms," once renowned as gathering places for intellectuals, evolved into cabarets, providing entertainment and mediocre food along with a steady supply of homemade red wine, thanks to the area's large Italian population.

The illegal beverage consumption was hidden behind closed doors and shuttered windows. Patrons were scrutinized from behind front door peepholes, admitted by tough guys who were always on the alert for raids by the vice squads. With money ready, these guys paid off the police. The demand for quality liquor gave rise to "bootleggers," the dispensers of illegal American-made spirits, and to smuggling, as gangsters imported spirits from Canada and abroad for distribution in the U.S.

Speakeasy owners found themselves millionaires practically overnight, with business obligations that could best be handled by professional strong-arm men. The result was termed organized crime, as these gangsters provided protection for their clubs, sharing part of the profits with local politicians to keep the vice squads away. Meanwhile, New York's vice squad was laughingly known as the training class for the best new bootleggers, as federal agents gave up their civil servant salaries in exchange for fortunes reaped by joining the other side of the law. The work was just as dangerous, but the pay was better. Besides, a vice agent-turned-bootlegger already had contacts with politicians, knew all the competitors, and knew what actions might be coming next from the federal government.

Thanks to liquor, Greenwich Village was suddenly a destination; its cabarets filled not just by its local residents, but by anyone seeking excitement, which Village clubs notoriously provided. It was a sexual meeting ground, where fantasy clubs were decorated like pirate's dens, prison cells, and country barns. It was a place where gay people could congregate in relative comfort.

Entrepreneurs soon realized that clandestine operations could generate more income with other forms of "entertainment." A

blacksmith's shop with its primary entrance in Pamela Court at 58 Barrow Street became Chumley's, with a secret, unmarked door around the corner (86 Bedford Street) for patrons to escape if (and when) the bar was raided for selling illegal spirits.

However, the secret speakeasy was actually a cover for the even more furtive casino upstairs. A dumbwaiter large enough to transport two adults at a time led from Chumley's kitchen to the second floor of 58 Barrow Street, where gamblers placed their bets into the wee hours.

"Legs" Diamond, 1931

Old real estate was put to new use, generating even greater profit. During Prohibition, Mayor Jimmy Walker, a celebrated reveler himself, debated with the Board of Estimate about removing the residential zoning from either 52nd or 55th Street to accommodate the dining needs of theatergoers.

After contemplation, they stripped the residential zoning from both streets. The once-elegant brownstones soon housed scores of speakeasies on lower floors, while upper levels were divided into flats populated by kept women, gigolos, more than one brothel, and the alleged residence of mobster "Legs" Diamond.

The 21 Club (at 21 West 52nd Street, then called Jack and Charlie's) hid over 5,000 cases of booze behind a trick basement wall where it remained undetected by authorities. Fifty-second Street soon became known simply as "The Street." Jazz musicians hopped from one speakeasy to another, while celebrities such as Jimmy Durante, George Murphy, and Ruby Keeler performed in smoky bars. The value of real estate in the West 50s skyrocketed.

Meanwhile, black Harlem became a congested place bursting

with street life. As parties simmered down in the speakeasies of the West 50s, Harlem clubs were picking up steam. Large cabarets like the Savoy Ballroom and the Cotton Club featured dazzling entertainers that defined the Jazz Age, from Duke Ellington's band to magnificent vocalists like Bessie Smith, Ethel Waters, and Bill "Bojangles" Robinson. The proprietors, most of them white, paid plenty to keep from being raided for serving bootleg booze, a cost they passed on to their predominantly white patrons, who were only too ready to pay for memorable evenings in Harlem's netherworld.

Prohibition officially ended in 1932 when the federal government repealed its misguided amendment, but one final wallop redefined New York's political system. To celebrate Prohibition's repeal, Mayor Jimmy Walker led a "Beer Parade" down Fifth Avenue, his last public appearance before facing charges brought by New York Governor Franklin Roosevelt. In previous months, a succession of Walker administration officials had difficulty explaining how their modest salaries generated personal fortunes, upon which taxes were often unpaid. Even Thomas Farley, the sheriff of New York County, couldn't explain how he amassed nearly a half-million dollars in six years on an annual salary of $8,500.

In courtroom testimony, it became apparent that not only were city officials accepting graft while permitting the sale and consumption of alcohol, but in the process, they accepted payoffs for just about everything else. Add an extra floor to a skyscraper without a variance? Just slip $3,000 to the Buildings Inspector. Dock a transatlantic ocean liner on a Hudson River pier? Pay $50,000 in unmarked bills. After

The Cotton Club

Duke Ellington and his band, c. 1925

months of courtroom wrangling and media scandal, Mayor Walker
resigned from office, Governor Roosevelt ran for President, and the
new mayor, Fiorello La Guardia, cleaned up much of the corruption
within New York City's government.

Now legal, most speakeasies simply removed the peepholes
from their front doors and openly welcomed the paying public.
With easy access to legal liquor, white patrons were less inclined to
visit Harlem, where clubs faded away, street congestion diminished,
and rents were reduced as supply exceeded demand. The effects of
Prohibition were felt for decades, but fortunately, today in New York,
it's not that exciting to buy a friend a drink.

① Chumley's
58 Barrow St.

❷ 21 Club
21 W. 52nd St.

③ Savoy Ballroom: Lenox Avenue
between W. 140th and W. 141st sts.

④ Cotton Club
W. 142nd St. and Lenox Ave.

Key for Map
❶ Current location
⓪ Site no longer exists

CHAPTER 21

A HARLEM HISTORY
PHILIP A. PAYTON, JR.
BUILDS A NEIGHBORHOOD

1902–1933

There is probably no real estate broker anywhere in twentieth-century America who has done more to develop a neighborhood, advance a cause, and launch a culture than Philip A. Payton, Jr. The neighborhood was Harlem at the turn of the twentieth century; Payton was the visionary who encouraged its development into America's preeminent black community. But let's start at the beginning.

Harlem wasn't always a black enclave. Originally settled in 1658 by Peter Stuyvesant under Dutch rule, Nieuw Haarlem was lush agricultural land distinctly separate from Nieuw Amsterdam at Manhattan's southern tip. For generations, the sole connection between the settlements was a diagonal road built on an old Indian path: today's Broadway. Following the War of 1812, agriculture gave way to commerce as farms were divided into Manhattan's now-familiar grid of streets and avenues, connecting rural Harlem, at least on paper, to the busy city to its south.

With the opening of the Harlem Railroad in the 1830s, and the Second and Third Avenue Railroads in 1879 and 1880, hundreds of tenement apartments were erected east of Third Avenue and north of 100th Street. Removed from the primary business hub downtown, Harlem residents made a compromise: spend nearly two hours each day on the trains, in an era when people routinely worked twelve hours per day, six days a week, in exchange for lower rents and an escape from the overcrowded tenements downtown. While the fare from the Battery to Harlem was fifteen cents each way, a special "rush hour" fare of seven cents was offered to commuters between five-thirty and seven a.m. and again in the evening from five to seven. It worked. Apartment houses built on speculation were soon filled with new residents. The once-sparse landscape blossomed into a desirable new "suburb" of Jewish, Italian, German, and Irish immigrants. When vaudeville impresario Oscar Hammerstein built the Harlem Opera House on 125th Street in 1889, Harlem became a destination.

As word got out in 1902 that the Interborough Rapid Transit would open subway stations along Harlem's west side, speculative builders wasted no time. Avoiding the low-rent tenements of Harlem's east side, many builders opted for grander and costlier dwellings: luxury apartment houses with elevators; spacious townhouses with marble mantels and parquet floors. Soon after

the grand subway opening of 1904, those builders were clobbered by harsh reality: in their zeal to develop Harlem's west side, they had over-estimated the market. The supply of residential real estate was far greater than its demand. New apartments and

34th Street and Broadway, 1911

townhouses stood half-empty while real estate taxes and mortgage repayments squeezed speculator's cash flow. Harlem was a real estate bust.

Meanwhile, a small black population settled in the area near Greeley Square at 34th Street and Broadway. With the arrival of Macy's and Gimbels department stores, residential buildings were being demolished to accommodate the new shopping district. The black residents were forced to move: never an easy prospect, since landlords throughout New York could legally refuse to

Philip A. Payton, Jr.

rent to people of color. Enter Philip Payton, a black man succeeding as a professional real estate broker in an era when African-Americans regularly faced discrimination in employment. Learning of the black families' plights and observing the empty properties in Harlem, Payton made the deal that changed Manhattan. He convinced financially strapped landlords to accept "colored" residents. He then led low-income black families to spacious new homes in Harlem, places they could not afford, and convinced them to double up, or sublet an extra room or two to make ends meet.

Landlords begrudgingly viewed Payton's plan as the only solution to their cash-flow crunch, especially when Payton extracted higher rents from his black tenants than landlords would get from whites. Tenants, too, had to get used to the idea of an extra boarder in their midst, but faced with limited choices in housing, Payton's economic balance worked. In the process, the black residents of Harlem developed a close-knit community. Within a decade, Harlem became one of the most densely populated areas in the entire nation.

In 1920, there were about 150,000 African-Americans living in New York and 100,000 of them lived in Harlem. By 1929, New York's black population had exploded to 327,000. Payton prospered, buying property on 134th Street at Fifth Avenue that he developed into housing for more black neighbors. Other landlords resisted. The

Seventh Avenue at West 125th Street, 1938

Kortright Apartments at 1990 Seventh Avenue, for example, didn't admit black tenants until 1926.

Rather than rent to dwindling numbers of white tenants, some landlords listed their buildings for sale; enterprising blacks pooled their resources and bought the buildings themselves. By 1925, African-Americans owned an estimated $60 million worth of Harlem real estate. Although the population boomed, the boundaries of the two-mile-long neighborhood barely expanded. As black neighborhoods became more densely populated, lines of segregation hardened.

In the years between the two World Wars, Harlem was filled with promise. Calling it "Dreamland" and "Black Mecca," entertainers touring America spoke with pride of the burgeoning community in Harlem. With soil exhaustion and the boll weevil pushing Southern blacks away from the land, Harlem became a destination of almost mythical proportions, where manufacturing jobs, a united community, and an escape from poll taxes and Jim Crow laws awaited. It was exotic, colorful, sensuous; a place that partied late into the night. The Cotton Club, Harlem's most exclusive nightspot, presented black headliners like Duke Ellington, Pearl Bailey and Lena Horne to a whites-only audience that was grateful for the bootleg liquor that accompanied its stellar entertainment.

Billie Holiday at Apollo Theater

However, for a mere forty cents at the door, dancers of all colors could swing all night in the Savoy Ballroom, to the sounds of jazz improvisers like Louis Armstrong, Earl Hines, and Coleman Hawkins. Elsewhere, tenants threw rent parties, paying anywhere from a dime to a half-dollar to cover a hard-luck-host's rent before the furniture landed on the sidewalk on the first of the month. Three-piece "pick-up bands," wailed their jazz through those dimly lit apartments, while amateur singers belted out popular radio songs. Some of the most gifted unemployed musicians of the 1930s played in Harlem's hallways, apartments and yards.

Harlem's success sparkled on brownstone streets like Strivers' Row (West 138th to 139th streets, between Adam Clayton Powell Jr. Boulevard and Frederick Douglass Boulevard), home to jazz pianist Eubie Blake, songwriter Noble Sissle, and W. C. Handy, the "Father of the Blues."

What ended the good times? In the Depression years, overcrowding and poverty were stifling. When Prohibition ended in 1933, Harlem's nightlife instantly declined. Clubs moved closer to their wealthier white patrons downtown; the music industry moved

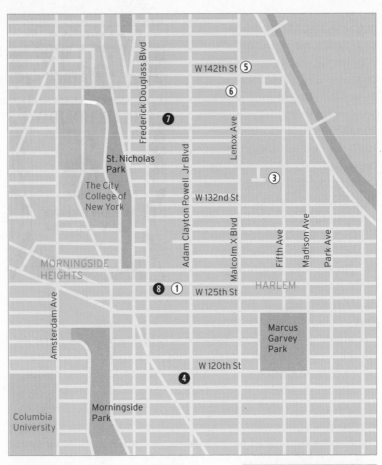

① Harlem Opera House: 207 W. 125th St.

❷ Greeley Square: W. 34th St. and Broadway

③ Philip Payton's Purchase: 134th St. at Fifth Ave.

❹ Kortright Apartments: 1990 Seventh Ave.

⑤ Cotton Club: W. 142nd Street and Lenox Avenue.

⑥ Savoy Ballroom
Lenox Ave. between W. 140th and W. 141st sts.

❼ Strivers' Row: W. 138th and W. 139th sts.

❽ Apollo Theater: 253 W. 125th St.

to Hollywood, and most jazz greats followed. Only a few clubs remained, like the Apollo Theater on 125th Street, now a testament to Harlem's durability.

Drug-related crimes drove away much of the population. By the 1970s, Harlem was again a real estate bust, with half-empty buildings wedged between prison-like housing projects.

But by the end of the twentieth century, Harlem reclaimed its status as a haven for real-estate buyers, families and young professionals. New shops and exciting clubs invited another generation to celebrate uptown, while investors of all colors restore Harlem's brownstones and its legacy. Be prepared, kids: The cost of train fare is no longer fifteen cents.

CHAPTER 22

THE MASTER BUILDER
THE CONTROVERSIAL
CHARACTER OF ROBERT MOSES

1924–1956

Imagine a highway running straight across SoHo, and the Village without Washington Square. Unthinkable.

These plans and many like them were real designs for Manhattan not so long ago. As New York's urban environment evolves to accommodate the demands of the lives and industries within it, urban planners sometimes conceived of wild notions in their efforts to fashion the best future for the city. For most of the twentieth century, a single mastermind dominated notions of urban design: Parks Commissioner Robert Moses. Admired and reviled, no strategist ever held more power or reshaped an American city as boldly. Moses' is an angry story of dreams, schemes, and tax dollars at work.

There is hardly a vista in any of New York's five boroughs that does not include Robert Moses' imprint. He built public works on a scale unmatched by any other individual in American history. By ramming bulkheads of steel beneath rivers and harbors, then

covering them with stone and cement, his teams created 15,000 acres of new land, permanently altering the physical boundaries of the city.

In Lower Manhattan, he approved public housing for 555,000 tenants (that's about the population of Wyoming), then built another giant complex, Co-op City, in the Bronx. He gave the city 658 playgrounds, 673 baseball diamonds, and 288 tennis courts; his convoys of trucks hauled the city's garbage into marshes that were then covered with earth and lawn to become more parks. From the Triborough Bridge (which was recently renamed after Robert F. Kennedy) to the Verrazano, plus Madison Square Garden, Lincoln Center, Shea Stadium and Jones Beach, Robert Moses brought his dreams to fruition. In the process, he evicted hundreds of thousands of New Yorkers from their homes, tore down buildings and constructed new ones according to his vision. Entire neighborhoods were obliterated at his command. Lives changed at his whim.

As a young attorney in 1924, Robert Moses met Governor Alfred E. Smith, who liked Moses' enthusiasm when discussing a new concept: a state park. Twenty-nine states didn't have any; six had one each. At the governor's suggestion, Moses drafted a bill establishing the Long Island State Park Commission, installing himself as president, then tackled his new assignment with vigor. With an increasing number of New Yorkers learning to drive, Moses noted that New York's streets were designed for horses and carriages. No major American city had expressways to accommodate rapid transit. If New Yorkers were ever to visit a state park on Long Island, there would have to be a State Parkway first. After months of tramping across sand spits and Long Island woodlands, Robert Moses mapped out a system of state parks covering 40,000 acres, linked by broad parkways to New York City. He was soon embroiled in years of scrappy vendettas against wealthy Long Island property owners, while acquiring land for the parkways through eminent domain, the legal concept that empowers the government to acquire privately owned land for public use. Those battles were forgiven when the magnificent Jones Beach State Park opened in 1929.

The press and public hailed Moses' vision; architects from Europe praised Jones Beach as "the finest seashore playground ever given the public anywhere in the world." More importantly, businesses clamored for locations near those parkway exits, spawning new construction, more jobs, and yes, new tax revenues for towns across Long Island. Politicians and schoolchildren alike cheered for Mr. Moses.

Robert Moses, 1939

In 1933, Mayor La Guardia invited Robert Moses to work his magic in New York City. Moses' reply: he would become the city's first Parks Commissioner only if he could also control its parkways and keep his state job.

With the governor and every local politician watching, the mayor consented. Moses then drafted the Triborough Act, an authority so cunning that it's still studied in colleges today. Its passage empowered his Triborough Authority to issue forty-year bonds to underwrite new bridges, parks, and roadways, with one clever catch: the existence of the Triborough Authority "shall continue only until its bonds have been paid in full." However, "The authority shall have power to refund any bonds by the issuance of new bonds, whether the bonds to be refunded have or have not matured, [to be used] for any other corporate purpose."

In other words, bonds would never mature, because the Authority would simply reissue those bonds, which were technically "new" for another forty years. As long as there were

The original Pennsylvania Station, 1962

bonds outstanding, the Triborough Authority remained in business, and so did Commissioner Moses. Further, as president of the Authority, Moses was completely autonomous; no City Council could shut him down, no mayor or governor could fire him, yet Robert Moses held the power throughout New York City and State to condemn housing, displace people, reshape the landscape, add highways, and build parks. He was soon the most prolific builder in Depression-weary America, with staggering amounts of money at his disposal.

It worked wonders. New York City needed a bridge connecting Manhattan to the Bronx but lacked the funds to build it. Waiting for a federal loan or raising tax money during the Depression would take years. Thanks to his track record, Robert Moses's Triborough Authority raised over $5 million in ten weeks through bond issues, and built the Henry Hudson Bridge. The interest and amortization on those bonds cost $370,000 annually. If every car crossing the bridge paid ten cents at the tollbooth, the Authority needed 3.7 million cars to meet the annual debt. In 1938, over ten million cars crossed the Henry Hudson Bridge, in 1939 almost thirteen million. Even with salaries and maintenance expenses, the revenue from that bridge was wildly successful, forcing the Authority to retire its forty-year bonds in less than a decade, issuing new ones while reaping millions annually to be spent on "any other corporate purpose." And that's just one bridge. Naturally, the Authority built six more. No New Yorker loved the automobile more than Robert Moses, and he didn't even drive.

Drunk with power, Moses took to the streets, building every major highway in New York, from the Harlem River Drive to the Gowanus Expressway; sixteen in all, each providing more bonds and more toll money. With such success, banks were quick to make loans to the Authority. The federal government provided funds as well, for urban renewal projects and roadway developments, which the Triborough Authority spent throughout the city. For example, $180 million was spent to add 132 acres of landfill along Riverside Drive, creating Riverside Park and the West Side Highway. Upon its opening, the *Journal-American* pronounced the park "a fountain of health and pleasure;" the *Daily News* hailed the West Side Highway "the most beautiful drive in the world."

But not all of Moses' ideas met such praise. He angered many residents by demolishing magnificent Penn Station and shoehorning Madison Square Garden between an office tower and the basement railroad station. He overrode their fury as he constructed Park Avenue South, razing buildings and displacing people to extend Park Avenue down to Union Square. His next plan: do the same thing to Fifth Avenue, tearing up historic Washington Square and the center of Greenwich Village to create Fifth Avenue South, a tony address, he assured his detractors, which would attract luxury residential development and increased tax revenues. Village neighbors, known worldwide for their activism, gathered in protest. Meanwhile, Moses planned a Lower Manhattan Expressway, connecting the Holland Tunnel to the Williamsburg and Manhattan bridges, which would tear up Broome Street and destroy hundreds of historic cast-iron buildings. Uptown, he proposed to "renew" the west side between Central Park and Broadway by demolishing its brownstones, to be replaced by blocks of new high-rises.

However, the tide of public opinion officially turned against him on April 17, 1956, over an unlikely project: the parking lot at the Tavern on The Green. The Parks Commissioner planned to tear up a section of Central Park used by West Side mothers with pre-school children to provide more space for cars. Well-heeled and well connected, these mothers watched the arrival of surveyors and bulldozing equipment, then contacted the press. Within hours, radio stations were telling listeners of the mothers' success at facing down a bulldozer with their baby carriages. Evening news broadcasts on television confirmed the images, only to be repeated in the next morning's newspapers. Humiliated by a week of editorials decrying the "mothers' battle to keep the grassy, wooded section a haven for their children," on April 24, Moses counterattacked before dawn. He summoned a platoon of uniformed park rangers to protect the bulldozer operators as they destroyed Central Park trees at 3 a.m. The outraged press went wild, running front-page photos of weeping mothers physically restrained by policemen while ax-wielding workmen ravaged Central Park.

Courtroom upheavals dogged Moses and the Triborough Authority for years, as scandals were exposed involving organized crime, questionable finance, and inaccurate reporting. Commissioner Moses, who once held twelve posts simultaneously within the city and state, met his match when Governor Nelson Rockefeller installed his brother Laurance as Moses' statewide replacement.

The Landmarks Preservation Commission was established in 1965 to ensure that New York would never lose another Penn Station. In 1969, Mayor John Lindsay designated Greenwich Village as the largest landmark district anywhere in the United States, followed by the formation of Friends of Cast-Iron Architecture in 1970, to protect the architecture of SoHo. The dynamo who started his public-service career so promisingly saw it end as politicians sidelined his wild notions for the streets of New York. Three mayors needed decades to devise a safer system of checks and balances for developing and maintaining New York's infrastructure.

Still, the victory belongs to Robert Moses. No city on earth grew at New York's rate under his leadership. Urban planners from every major city in America sought his advice on contracts, designs, personnel, and finance, yet none could amass the volume of work Moses accomplished in service to New York. His bridges, beaches, parks, and parkways are a legacy to be used, enjoyed and admired for generations.

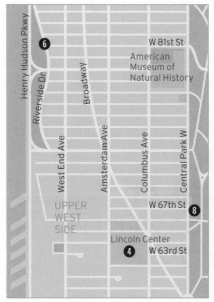

① Proposed Lower Manhattan
   Expressway

❷ Triborough Bridge

❸ Madison Square Garden

❹ Lincoln Center

❺ Harlem River Drive

❻ Riverside Park and the West Side
   Highway

⑦ The Original Penn Station

❽ Tavern on The Green

Key for Map

❶ Current location

① Site no longer exists

CHAPTER 23

MANHATTAN HEARS THE BEAT
HOW A GROUP OF WRITERS CHANGED NEW YORK

1944–1963

America was thrilled when World War II ended. After all, the boys were back; new chapters could begin in squeaky-clean suburbs as society attempted to dismiss inner-city squalor, the emerging drug trade, and rising racial tensions.

As prosperous whites moved away from Manhattan, the population of poor people increased; 375,000 blacks arrived between 1940 and 1960, and the number of Puerto Rican immigrants quadrupled. During this transition, a group of radicals emerged with a decidedly different view of the postwar world, determined to explore America's underside and report their discoveries. From the intellectual pursuits at Columbia University and the carnal pursuits of Times Square and bohemian Greenwich Village, these outspoken writers gave birth to the Beat Generation, a movement that started in the streets of Manhattan but soon commanded the attention of an international audience.

The movement got off to a strange start when seventeen-year-old Columbia freshman Allen Ginsberg and fellow student Lucien Carr headed to 48 Morton Street to visit David Kammerer, Carr's former teacher from St. Louis. Ginsberg, contemplating his homosexual orientation in an era when such things could barely be whispered, wrote that he was "going down to the Village where all the fairies were. It was both romantically glorious, and at the same time frightening and frustrating." A week later, he and Carr headed back downtown to 69 Bedford Street to meet Carr's friend William S. Burroughs, another St. Louis native, a writer by day and bartender by night. Soon after, Carr introduced these friends to football-star-turned-college-dropout Jack Kerouac, who lived with his girlfriend near the Columbia campus. A life-altering twist created a bond that the friends never anticipated: After a night of drinking in the West End Bar on Broadway at 114th Street, Kammerer made a pass at his former student Carr in Riverside Park; Carr stabbed him twice in the heart with a Boy Scout knife, killing him. Kerouac hid the knife while Burroughs escorted Carr to the police. When Kammerer's body was found floating in the Hudson off 108th Street, Kerouac and Burroughs were arrested as material witnesses, Carr pleaded guilty to manslaughter and served two years in prison.

The lurid tale catapulted their names and faces onto the front pages of all seven of New York's daily newspapers. When Ginsberg submitted one chapter about the incident to his teacher, Columbia's dean expressly forbade him to write further. The message was plain: Kerouac, Burroughs, and Ginsberg didn't fit within America's wholesome vision of college boys. They were outlaws.

That wasn't a tough position for up-and-coming writers. The three soon shared an apartment together at 419 West 115th Street. With Burroughs as their leader they found excitement in Times Square, hanging out in all-night bars with jazz musicians and servicemen, as well as hustlers, junkies, and prostitutes. The trio shared the belief that great secrets lurked at America's heart, and that personal transcendence might be found if they dared to explore the nation's soul. While politicians touted America's new prosperity, declaring American life to be the standard to which the world should aspire, Ginsberg, Kerouac, and Burroughs were arriving at a different conclusion. Despite the nation's victories abroad, there were many battles to be waged at home, specifically minority rights, and later gay rights.

Times Square

These young writers listened to the music of bebop, sampled marijuana and recreational drugs, and observed that a new world still largely underground was being born. In the streets of Manhattan, they presided over the first counterculture movement to have a major impact on America's popular culture.

Herbert Huncke, a junkie hustler they met in Times Square referred to them as "beat," meaning beat down, or wasted. Kerouac heard additional possibilities in the word "beat," referring to a new cadence for speech and writing, and the new rhythms of jazz. The authors' works gained recognition and publication at about the time Russia launched its Sputnik satellite into orbit. Noting the leftist leanings of Kerouac, Ginsberg, and Burroughs, one witty reviewer lifted the "nik" from Sputnik, referring to the writers as beatniks. The label came to define a movement as well as an entire generation and a Manhattan neighborhood.

That beatnik neighborhood, of course, was Greenwich Village, though the writers could only afford to live on its periphery. Ginsberg first maintained an apartment at 346 West 15th Street, where he wrote the poems for his book *Empty Mirror*. He frequented the San Remo Cafe at 93 MacDougal Street, which soon attracted

Actor Montgomery Clift, far left, and Jack Kerouac, far right, eat at the San Remo Cafe.

avant-garde artists Jackson Pollock, Willem de Kooning, composer John Cage, choreographer Merce Cunningham and many others. Village bars and coffee houses near Washington Square exploited their presence, attempting to cash in on New York's beatnik scene.

What did the Beat writers accomplish that provoked such interest? They wrote in a new, direct way that has influenced writers ever since. William S. Burroughs wrote his acclaimed *Naked Lunch* by forging a new "cut-up" writing technique, forcing the reader to accept short phrases as complete thoughts, simulating a rapid-fire thought process in printed form.

Allen Ginsberg claimed that he heard a prophetic voice telling him to "cultivate the terror, get right into it." From that inspiration came *Howl*, a stream-of-consciousness poem about the discarded dreams and discarded people in America. At a gallery event, with Kerouac sitting on the floor tapping rhythms on a wine jug and chanting "Go, go, go," Ginsberg read *Howl* to instant and unanimous acclaim, the first work of the era to speak for the outcasts. As a result, poetry readings became emblematic gatherings across Greenwich Village. Upon publication, *Howl* was deemed obscene; Ginsberg's words were put on trial. Following a climactic defense, Ginsberg was vindicated in court; a living American poet was suddenly famous.

Jack Kerouac crisscrossed America by car for three years with his pal Neal Cassady, two modern swashbucklers risking adventure. Early in April 1951, Kerouac taped together rolls of twenty-foot-long Japanese writing paper, then fed one end into his typewriter. Fueled by coffee and Benzedrine, he wrote of his adventures, taking little time to sleep. Kerouac finished *On the Road* by April 22nd: 86,000 words on a 120-foot roll. Written as one single paragraph with almost no punctuation, the prose "comes at you just as the road comes at you." Blinded by the deviant characters the two antiheroes encounter, no publisher would touch the manuscript, fearing the scrutiny of Senator Joseph McCarthy's Un-American Activities Committee. Following *Howl*'s courtroom battle, Allen Ginsberg championed Kerouac's novel, which was finally published in 1957. It is hailed today as a modern masterpiece.

The Beat era ended in New York for two reasons. Ginsberg, Kerouac and Burroughs saw their works trivialized as mainstream America wrestled to accept their gritty material. By 1958, the Village was overrun by weekend beatniks in berets and goatees. This superficiality reached its zenith in Maynard G. Krebs, a beatnik character on TV's *The Many Loves of Dobie Gillis*; he provided comic relief with no sting or relevance to the Beats' New Vision.

More importantly, the assassination of President John F. Kennedy proved the Beats' point: there were darker secrets lurking in white-bread America after all. That catalytic moment in 1963 pointed rebellious writers in a new direction: hippiedom, as hippies soon replaced beatniks in Washington Square with new issues to challenge. Ideas initiated by the Beat Generation exploded into a new social awareness felt around the world.

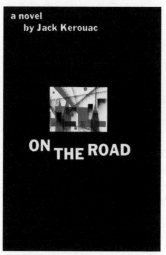

On the Road, first edition, 1967

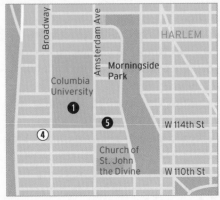

1. Columbia University

2. David Kammerer's apartment
48 Morton St.

3. William S. Burroughs' house
69 Bedford St.

4. West End Bar
Broadway at W. 114th St.

5. Kerouac/Burroughs/Ginsberg
apartment: 419 W. 115 St.

6. Times Square

7. Ginsberg writes *Empty Mirror*
346 W. 15th St.

8. San Remo Cafe
93 MacDougal St.

9. Washington Square Park

Key for Map
0 Current location
0 Site no longer exists

CHAPTER 24

SOHO STORY
A NEIGHBORHOOD GROWS
1960s–1980s

The nineteenth-century cast-iron buildings that make up the
neighborhood south of Washington Square were subjects of
contention in the twentieth century. Their bumpy transition
from a collection of grimy iron buildings into a chic Manhattan
neighborhood is a story of determination.

By the 1950s and '60s, New Yorkers had just about forgotten
the buildings south of Houston Street. Up in Greenwich Village,
home to many successful artists, landlords pocketed top dollar as
tenants squeezed into tiny apartments. A short walk away, a spacious
industrial section sat fallow; its zoning required landlords to rent
only to small businesses in need of workspace. However, most of
the garment-related businesses that once populated the area had
relocated their machinery to the West 30s decades earlier to escape
the fire-prone wooden floors within those cast-iron buildings. Even
Ladies' Mile packed up and moved to larger shops above 14th Street.
South of Houston Street was Manhattan's forgotten enclave.

New York City's Planning Commissioner, Robert Moses, thought he had the solution: tear down the aging and unprofitable cast-iron buildings to make way for a Lower Manhattan Expressway. He proposed that a highway cut through the heart of the neighborhood, on Broome Street, linking the Holland Tunnel with the Williamsburg and Manhattan bridges.

Meanwhile, the art scene was changing. Contemporary artists like Jackson Pollock and Mark Rothko sold paintings that were larger than some apartment walls. They required large spaces in which to create these works. Greenwich Village artists just couldn't afford to stretch huge canvases in tight spaces and meet those Village rents. They had to find a better space.

Artists like Alex Katz, Jeff Koons, Jean-Michel Basquiat, David Salle, and Julian Schnabel landed south of Houston Street and famously went to work. The ambience seemed to breed success; soon everyone dreamed of life in an edgy SoHo loft. Those pioneering artists provoked a firestorm that took decades to quell— as politicians, landlords, manufacturers, bureaucrats, lawyers and brokers flexed their muscles to assume control over the rediscovered neighborhood.

First, that highway proposal had to be defeated. When local artists joined forces with a group of preservationists including Jane Jacobs, James Marston Fitch, and Margot Gayle, activists discovered a new synergy when tackling City Hall. The city government agreed to save its money and retract its highway plans.

The next glitch: to relocate south of Houston Street, artists had to sign commercial leases for large workspaces, foregoing the protection of rent control, the laws that govern how much the landlords could raise rents on residential units.

Artists would now live and work in a single flat, not unlike their forebears at the Tenth Street Studios some fifty years earlier; a radical concept to most New Yorkers. Despite the commercial zoning, landlords looked the other way, pleased to see their buildings occupied again, seldom warning artists that to sleep in a commercial space was a violation of the law. It became the personal expense of

SoHo pioneers to make those commercial lofts habitable; what an artist saved on rent went into long-term investments in kitchens, bathtubs, hot water tanks, and space heaters.

Unlike commercial tenants who moved from one address to another as rents and business evolved, artists brought their families and moved in to stay. Enterprising landlords saw their neighborhood's appeal among the avant garde and cashed in. When the commercial leases expired, renewals were offered sometimes at quadruple the initial rent. The artists were being priced out of the area they made desirable.

The artists joined forces and complained to the city government, as did the landlords, whose rent increases were perfectly legal. Longtime tenants who rented space for manufacturing complained bitterly too, for the higher rents would "drive them from the borough," taking employment opportunities elsewhere. Mayor John Lindsay stepped into the fray. Initially elected as a Republican, Lindsay might have been expected to support the landlord's position, since it was they who paid the real estate taxes on the buildings at stake. Instead, Lindsay simply counted heads. There were more tenants than landlords. He would maintain his popularity when seeking re-election by supporting the tenants against their landlords. In subsequent elections, Lindsay never ran for office again as a Republican.

To guarantee affordable lofts, Mayor Lindsay envisioned an artist's commune in SoHo. To avoid displacing the manufacturers, Lindsay decided there was no need to change the zoning, since artists were technically "manufacturing"

Broadway, north from Prince Street, 1904

Cast-iron Architecture

I n 1848 industrial inventor James Bogardus proposed a solution to New York City's "housing problem." While traveling in England, he became enamored of the cast-iron facades used in the construction of bridges, aqueducts and the interiors of market halls and libraries. Determined to introduce the concept in America, he specified that the exterior of his new factory at Duane and Centre streets in downtown Manhattan be made

of identical, pre-cast metal panels fabricated by pouring liquid iron into shapely molds. In far less time than it took masons to build a standard exterior, these panels would then be bolted to a brick interior wall. Soon, Bogardus had two foundries working overtime casting these panels.

The introduction of cast iron revolutionized structural engineering. In traditional multi-story construction, the walls on the ground floor needed extra thickness to support the weight of the walls above. The taller the building, the thicker the walls were at street-level. Invariably, this was at the expense of otherwise-valuable retail space. Not so with cast iron. Buildings partially made of brick and paneled in cast-iron became slimmer, taller, airier and more spacious. Street floors were transformed into wide panes of glass interspersed with tall slender columns that held up the buildings. Of course, the wide windows were perfect for displays of commercial goods; the term "window-shopping" came into vogue at this time.

Despite its practicality, cast-iron construction fell from grace with the

arrival of steel. The invention of a metal even stronger than cast-iron caused architects to rethink basic construction concepts. Instead of relying on exterior walls of brick, stone, or iron to support a building, steel beams made a rigid interior superstructure possible, supporting enormous weight.

In the zeal to make the city taller, cast-iron buildings fell to the wrecking ball. Those that survived became derelicts once the old garment district moved uptown. In August 1973, passage of a local landmark preservation law led to the federally backed National Historic Landmark designation for SoHo in June 1978. Today, 139 iron-front buildings on twenty-six city blocks of SoHo and scattered buildings in TriBeCa represent the largest collection of cast-iron buildings in the world. A stroll along Mercer Street, Greene Street, lower Broadway or Lafayette Street looks much as it did 100 years ago. Only the trees have been added.

art. In 1971 he devised the Department of Cultural Affairs with Bess Myerson, the former Miss America, as its Commissioner, overseeing a new Artist-in-Residence (A.I.R.) District, which roughly encompassed Broadway to West Broadway, Houston Street to Canal Street. To live and work from a single unit in this prime district, residents had to prove they were artists, and secure an Artist-in-Residence Certificate from the Department of Cultural Affairs.

Pioneering art dealer Paula Cooper opened the first gallery in SoHo in 1968 on Prince Street. Ivan Karp, a former director of the Leo Castelli Gallery opened O.K. Harris Gallery on West Broadway in 1969. Enormously successful and influential, Castelli opened a downtown branch of his gallery in 1971 at 420 West Broadway, a building that eventually housed multiple galleries, becoming one of the prime gallery venues in New York City. Not all of the artists he represented were thrilled. Roy Lichtenstein, Castelli recalled, "told me that nobody will ever go there."

To maintain its character, the neighborhood needed new artists. The affordability of living and working lofts would be preserved only as long as resident artists sold their lofts to other artists. That logic worked for a few years, while real estate prices remained stable. However, as the real estate boom of the early 1980s worked its magic, artists turned out to be just as profit-minded as their former landlords. Artists in residence could no longer afford to think of selling lofts for their modest acquisition costs because they couldn't afford the prices outside SoHo. New artists would have to pay competitive market prices, or SoHo would stagnate.

To acquire a certificate from the Department of Cultural Affairs, an artist needed to present a portfolio of work along with proof of income from art. Some non-artists, who didn't qualify for the certificate, built lofts in the triangle-below-Canal Street instead. That TriBeCa neighborhood delivered loft living to anyone willing to pay the price, as SoHo denizens quickly recognized. With the city government restricting SoHo resales to the certificate holders, TriBeCa became the desirable place, driving the price of a downtown loft. Such well-known artists as Keith Haring and Red Grooms bought lofts just beyond the A.I.R. District.

That's when things got ugly. The arcane legalities required to buy a SoHo loft remained one of the New York City government's best-kept secrets. With civil servants determining who made art, the cutting-edge district was soon populated by people simply clever enough to beat the system. Wealthy professionals who were married to artists built SoHo pleasure palaces thanks to the spouse's mediocre-but-certifiable attempts at art. Or the rental trick: non-artists bought a full floor, apportioned a small section of it to be rented to an artist and then developed the remainder for themselves. Actor Wesley Snipes, for example, moved into an artist's loft as a subtenant since acting wasn't recognized as an art by the Department of Cultural Affairs, despite Snipes' celebrated career. Every downtown broker can share a similar war story.

The Department of Cultural Affairs finally had to loosen its restraints. In the late 1980s, savvy developers realized that by selling lofts as condominiums, and fully disclosing that while the building was located within the A.I.R. District, they could sell to anyone willing to sign a waiver. This indemnified the seller from any action that might be taken by the Department of Cultural Affairs. In a cost-cutting gesture, Mayor Rudy Giuliani's administration significantly reduced the size of the Department, disbanding the panel that once scrutinized applicant portfolios.

The original artists of SoHo watched their neighborhood evolve far beyond the original plan for an art community. Then they joyfully cashed the walloping checks from a newer generation who paid retail for the privilege of owning a small piece of SoHo. The demand hasn't subsided. Visitors from around the world are attracted to the stylish boutiques and trendy clubs within historic buildings. SoHo's once-grimy buildings, molded in iron, are now protected as national landmarks.

Downtown Triangle Completes A Circle

The triangle of land below Canal Street has been known as TriBeCa since the 1970s, but it was called Washington Market for far longer, starting soon after the Civil War. The South Street Seaport on the East River was too small to accommodate America's rapidly expanding shipping industry, so business shifted to the Hudson River on Manhattan's West side, where more piers could meet the demands of the trade boom.

Washington Market, 1936

The city government supported the process by building its Retail Market, a block-square bourse between Fulton and Vesey streets on West Street, filled with stalls for produce vendors. In 1869, when Commodore Vanderbilt erected a freight terminal for his New York Central Railroad at nearby Laight Street, the neighborhood was plainly defined as New York's export center. For decades, a pedestrian couldn't even see the expansive Hudson River, as freighters and steamships occupied every inch of the waterfront.

The Washington Market was a noisy, smelly, congested free-for-all, with trains overhead, trucks lurching toward tunnels and four ferry terminals, while vendors hawked their wares in the cold, salty air or beside all-night bonfires. By 1935, the industry within those several blocks accounted for a whopping twenty-two percent of the entire nation's export trade, equaling the trade statistics of Boston, Philadelphia, San Francisco, and Chicago combined. The speed at which goods could now travel within America, thanks to rapid freight trains, meant that dairy products

that can easily spoil could be shipped quickly from this central hub.

When Charles "Lucky Lindy" Lindbergh crossed the Atlantic in an airplane, exporters witnessed their future. By the end of World War II, most industries had packed and moved to the close proximity of airfreight hangars. The ferries stopped, train tracks were dismantled, the terminals were closed, the City demolished the Retail Market, and an entire neighborhood disappeared.

And that was the best thing that could have happened. Rambling storehouses with high ceilings turn out to make terrific homes. With architecture similar to that of SoHo, TriBeCa was ripe for expansion as loft living gained in popularity.

Non-artists in the late 1970s avoided the complications of the Artist-In-Residence process by renovating the mostly-empty warehouses just south of SoHo, where free-market prices prevailed. Celebrities carved out fantasy lofts tucked away from uptown tour buses. World-class restaurants moved in, and families brought the joyful sounds of permanent residence. The Washington Market lives again.

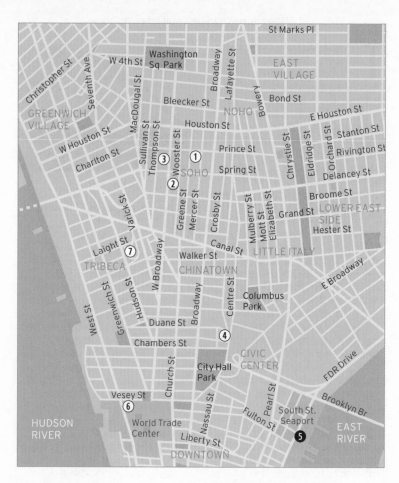

① Paula Cooper Gallery
(1968 until 1996)
96 Prince St.

② OK Harris Gallery
383 West Broadway

③ Leo Castelli Gallery
(1971 until 1999)
420 West Broadway

④ First cast-iron building
Duane St. at Centre St.

⑤ South Street Seaport

⑥ Retail Market
West St. between
Fulton and Vesey sts.

⑦ New York Central Railroad Terminal
Laight St.

CHAPTER 25

CHELSEA
THE WESTERN FRONTIER

1990–

When the popularity of SoHo priced out artists and even galleries in the 1990s, the creative crowd headed to the spacious warehouses in the westernmost reaches of Chelsea—the neighborhood west of Fifth Avenue bounded by 14th Street and 34th Street. For decades, those warehouses sat fallow, collecting minimal rents as the shipping industry relocated to southern California where Asian imports increased at a rapid rate.

Originally the sprawling farm of Clement Clarke Moore, author of *A Visit from St. Nicholas* (also known as *Twas the Night Before Christmas*), Chelsea's acreage was divided into city blocks in the early 1800s. The Moores donated one newly-designated block to the Presbyterian Church, on which it built the first seminary in America. To this day, the General Theological Seminary occupies the block from Ninth Avenue to Tenth Avenue from 20th to 21st streets, serving as the centerpiece of the Chelsea Landmark District. Residents may stroll its pastoral lawn, one of Chelsea's most

Clement Clarke Moore

romantic and best-kept secrets.

The area's rich history includes the infamous Chelsea Hotel on West 23rd Street, where many celebrated performers made their home. Bob Dylan, Janis Joplin, Leonard Cohen, Patti Smith, Iggy Pop and Tom Waits are among the musicians who lived here. It's where poet Dylan Thomas died, where Arthur C. Clarke wrote *2001: A Space Odyssey*, and where Nancy Spungen, girlfriend of Sex Pistols' bassist Sid Vicious, met her untimely death in 1978.

In the 1980s, when the Gay Men's Health Crisis opened on the ground floor of 318 West 22nd Street, Chelsea was already known as the largest enclave of gay men and lesbians in Manhattan; their investments in the gentrified neighborhood turned Chelsea into one of New York's most fashionable addresses, and property values soared. World-renowned architects like Frank Gehry made their mark on the neighborhood, developing a new landscape outside the landmark district that embraces the future without compromising its history. Those costly new residences with majestic views of the Hudson River became East Coast homes for many of Hollywood's biggest names, including Harrison Ford, Nicole Kidman, Calista Flockhart, and Ethan Hawke.

The once-empty pier buildings on the river found new uses, too. The Chelsea Piers serve as a film and television studio (NBC's *Law & Order* filmed there for over a decade), plus a sports complex including a skating rink and gymnastics center. Then in 2009 the High Line opened, an innovative elevated park built on the abandoned railroad tracks that once serviced the docks along the Hudson River. Cherished by locals and tourists alike, the High Line is a prime place to view the area's eclectic architectural past and present.

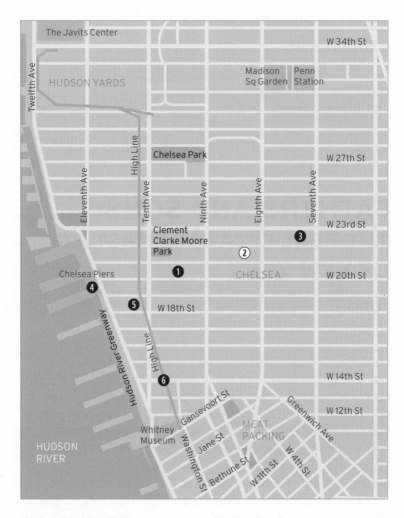

① General Theological Seminary

② Gay Men's Health Crisis
318 West 22nd St.

③ Chelsea Hotel
222 West 23rd St.

④ Chelsea Piers

⑤ IAC Center (Frank Gehry-designed)
555 West 18th St.

⑥ High Line Park

CHAPTER 26

FATHERS AND SONS
THE REAL ESTATE DYNASTIES
OF NEW YORK

1920–

Days after George Washington took the presidential oath, John Jacob Astor bought two lots on the Bowery for $625 cash. The profits he reaped were so alluring that future generations were groomed just to pass the torch. To most Americans in those days, Astor's first real estate transaction seemed like no bargain; after all, Peter Minuit supposedly bought the whole island of Manhattan for bunches of beads and $24 worth of Spanish-milled coins.

But to twenty-six-year-old Astor, that comparison clinched the deal: Manhattan's land values increased spectacularly, despite upheavals like the Revolution and the French and Indian War. To Mr. Astor, the profits from long-term investments made Manhattan real estate a terrific family business.

Many other patriarchs dreamed of a real estate dynasty, though not all met with Astor's success or intergenerational continuity. Over the years, Astor invested thousands, acquiring undeveloped lots throughout Lower Manhattan. Meanwhile, those profitable

Astor House Hotel, c. 1908

investments financed Astor's son William through Germany's best universities, where he learned to manage and invest the family's portfolio. When William joined his father's Manhattan firm in 1830, the senior Astor was the wealthiest man in the New World, with $2 million in real estate holdings. Soon after, grandson John Jacob Astor III joined the family business too.

As New York's population exploded, Astor taught the merits of density to his descendants, collecting multiple rents from a single address. On a strawberry patch that was later to be known as the Lower East Side, the Astors erected hundreds of tenement houses, soon packed with tens of thousands of European immigrants. The profits from those multiple units provided the capital to build the family's biggest moneymaker of all: the Astor House hotel on Broadway near City Hall. With 300 bedrooms at two dollars per night, the daily profits from the luxurious hotel guaranteed permanence for the Astor dynasty. In his old age, when John Jacob deeded the hotel to William for "one Spanish-milled dollar, with love and affection;" the Astor dynasty was conveyed between generations.

Outside the family, John Jacob Astor confided that his son William "will never make money, but he'll keep what he has." An accurate observation: During his years as head of the estate, William managed only to double its size, a growth rate of between two and three percent annually, compounded. The old man's insights characterized many other second-generation investors in dynasties to come: the nature of their tasks differed from the tasks of the founders. While John Jacob took great risks in Manhattan property and reaped an enormous fortune, that same fortune constrained William from being equally daring. The first Astor had nothing to lose; the second, everything.

The next generation of real estate moguls keenly observed the Astor family's path to success. As self-employed entrepreneurs, these new Americans took responsibilities for their successes or failures. They saved their cash to invest in income-producing properties for themselves and their future generations while New York continued to prosper.

One such character was A. E. Lefcourt, who made a living on the streets selling newspapers and shining shoes. While most paperboys were content with one route, the entrepreneurial Lefcourt secured additional jobs, then paid other boys to deliver the papers for him. As Lefcourt explained it, if he could sell shoe shines, he could sell anything. He soon became a salesman for a dress manufacturer. When the owner retired, Lefcourt bought the business, hired more salesmen, then diversified his assets into Manhattan real estate. Lefcourt knew the Lower East Side sweatshops first-hand; here, laborers risked their lives over primitive sewing machines that caused fires almost daily. Following the tragic Triangle Shirtwaist Factory fire in 1911, which sent 146 girls leaping out of windows to die on the Greene Street sidewalk, Lefcourt built the first loft building north of 34th Street, then encouraged other "needle trades" to move into safer buildings as well. In 1923, he formed his own construction company, assembled the major block fronts

Firemen search for victims of the Triangle Shirtwaist Factory fire, 1911

on Broadway and Eighth Avenue from 36th to 39th streets, and built today's Garment District. As manufacturers abandoned the downtown lofts that are some of today's trendiest residential addresses, Lefcourt's pioneering vision saved lives and earned him a fortune.

Best of all, Lefcourt had a son. On the occasion of Alan's bar mitzvah, Lefcourt deeded him a $10 million building at 34th Street and Madison Avenue. But the dreams of dynasties don't always work as planned. Five years later, in October 1929, Lefcourt announced plans to build the world's tallest building at Broadway and 49th Street, just weeks before the stock market crashed, sinking the country into the Great Depression. By February 1930, the boy was dead. The grieving Lefcourt scrapped his plans and built a modest eleven-story building instead. Over the entrance of the so-called Brill Building, Lefcourt placed a head-and-shoulders bust of his young son. Though A. E. Lefcourt is remembered as a prolific builder, there would be no Lefcourt dynasty.

Some sons forego the dynasty to seek other opportunities. By the time Joseph P. Kennedy Sr.'s career as Ambassador to Great Britain ended in 1941, he had amassed $30 million investing in Wall Street and Hollywood. With such a significant cash hoard, he easily secured bank loans at favorable rates and began to invest in real estate. Kennedy would buy a building for $1 million, mortgage it for eighty percent of its value at the low rate of four percent per year, reap six percent profit from its rents even before the building appreciated, then use the mortgage dollars as down payment on other properties. His timing and access to cash were ideal. He bought the corner of 51st Street and Lexington Avenue for $600,000, and sold it for nearly $4 million; the corner of 46th Street and Lexington Avenue, bought for $1.7 million, was sold not much later for nearly $5 million; the corner of 59th and Lexington Avenue, bought for $1.9 million with only $100,000 in cash was sold for $6 million. In one lucky decade, Joseph P. Kennedy, Sr. tripled his fortune.

Joseph P. Kennedy, Sr. 1939

And Kennedy, too, had sons. However, those sons, comparing their dad's career as a political ambassador against his activities as an investor, famously chose the former. Kennedy liquidated most of his real estate holdings in New York to concentrate his attention and encouragement to the political careers of his offspring.

Some sons surpass the achievements of the earlier generation, as is surely the case of Fred and Donald Trump. As the son of Swedish immigrants, Fred Trump trained as a carpenter. Working as a teenager to support his widowed mother, he built his first one-family house in Queens at age seventeen. During the Depression and World War II, Fred Trump completed 2,500 homes for the Federal Housing Administration, and parlayed his knowledge of government contracts into subsidized housing complexes in Bensonhurst and Brighton Beach in Brooklyn. However, Fred Trump was investigated twice by the FHA: once for borrowing more money to erect two complexes than it had cost to build them, then pocketing $1.6 million in dividends without FHA approval. (Trump was not alone. Norman Tishman faced a similar investigation in

John D. Rockefeller, Sr. and John D. Rockefeller, Jr., 1915

Rego Park.) A decade later, Trump was again scrutinized unfavorably, for contributing too generously to political officials as they sought re-election. As opposing candidates denounced his patronage, one politician was forced to resign from the city planning commission. Though the contributions were legal, laws were rewritten to prevent developers from getting too cozy with politicians.

Fred Trump's humiliation cemented young Donald's determination to get his father out of the subsidized housing industry and into prestigious projects. Soon after graduating from the University of Pennsylvania's esteemed Wharton School, he convinced his father to remortgage 24,000 apartments, a move that provided cash for the younger Trump's expansion. For the next five years, Donald bought and sold apartment complexes, building equity, then made an audacious move into Manhattan, striking a deal with the near-broke Penn Central Railroad.

It was Donald who taught Fred the value of high-profile transactions as he acquired the Commodore Hotel adjacent to Grand Central Terminal. Paying $10 million, Donald gained the government's concession of no property taxes for forty years. He then turned the dilapidated building into the sleek Grand Hyatt hotel, following the lead of the earliest Astors.

The publicity generated by that transaction was the attention for which Donald clamored. Soon he was being chauffeured around town like a movie star, socializing among the glitterati, reinventing the Trump name and establishing a dynasty as colorful as the Astors. Today, Trump is known across America for luxurious housing, and perhaps even more for his frequent television and tabloid appearances.

The most pensive lesson about a dynasty comes from the Rockefellers. After John D. Rockefeller, Sr., made his fortune in oil, his son John Jr. and grandson Nelson took great interest in developing today's Rockefeller Center, acres of real estate that are collectively hailed as one of Manhattan's greatest jewels. But within the Rockefeller dynasty, the steady income from the Center's investment proved insufficient, as subsequent generations stretched the family fortune to its limits. As the eighty-eight sons and daughters of Rockefellers dreamed their own entrepreneurial dreams, many inherited too little seed money to bring their ideas to fruition.

Making headline news on November 1, 1989, the fiftieth anniversary of Rockefeller Center, the dynasty sold its controlling interest to the Mitsubishi Company of Tokyo for $846 million. The sale deposited a huge cash infusion into the trusts from which the fifth-generation Rockefellers derive their income, empowering the youngest investors to realize their dreams.

The sale signaled the end of the Rockefeller's clout within Manhattan real estate, but opened exciting new doors. No longer constrained to maintaining the single fortune, the youngest generation scattered to begin their own dynasties, using the power of their family name to take new risks in multiple directions. And for that, Peter Minuit, John Jacob Astor, and fathers everywhere must share a knowing smile.

① Astor House Hotel
Broadway between
Vesey and Barclay sts.

❷ Triangle Shirtwaist Factory
Greene St. at Washington Pl.

❸ Brill Building
Broadway at W. 49th St.

❹ E. 51st St. and Lexington Ave.

❺ E. 46th St. and Lexington Ave.

⑥ E. 59th St. and Lexington Ave.

❼ Grand Hyatt hotel
109 E. 42nd St.

❽ Rockefeller Center

Map labels:
Central Park
Union Sq
W 14th St
Fifth Ave
University Pl
Greene St
MIDTOWN
MoMA
Park Ave
Lexington Ave
Third Ave
E 59th St
E 51st St
W 49th St Rockefeller Plaza
Washington Sq Park
GREENWICH VILLAGE
Broadway
Times Sq
E 46th St
Grand Central Terminal
W 42nd St
Bryant Park
NY Public Library
Fifth Ave
Madison Ave
Church St
Broadway
City Hall Park
Barclay St
Vesey St
Nassau St
World Trade Center
DOWNTOWN
W 34th St
Penn Station
Empire State Building
MURRAY HILL

OLD NEW YORK
WALKING TOURS

Visit the Places Where History Really Happened

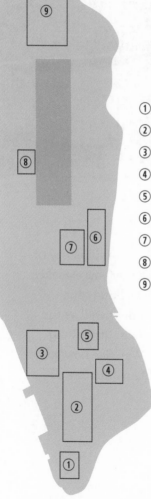

FINANCIAL DISTRICT

An epic chapter was added to the already-plentiful history of Lower Manhattan when the World Trade Center was attacked and destroyed on September 11, 2001. This walking tour includes a visit to the 9/11 Memorial Museum as well as the historic streets that surround it, with anecdotes stretching back to America before the Revolutionary War. See how some of New York's most modern architecture fits within one of America's earliest settlements.

Canal St

Walker St

White St

CHINATOWN

TRIBECA

Mulberry St

Mott St

Bayard St

Columbus Park

Division St

Leonard St

6 Ave

Worth St

Lafayette St

Henry St

Harrison St

Hudson St

Varick St

Duane St

Broadway

W Broadway

Centre St

Pearl St

Park Row

Madison St

St James St

Catherine St

Washington Market Park

Chambers St

Warren St

Murray St

City Hall Park

1
2

3

Franklin St

CIVIC CENTER

Park Pl

Park Row

5

Brooklyn Bridge

Church St

Barclay St

Vesey St

World Trade Center

9 **7** **6**

Nassau St

William St

Gold St

Fulton St

Pearl St

Water St

South St Seaport

12 **13**

10

John St

Maiden Ln

Liberty St

15 **11** **16** **17**

26 **28**

Fletcher St

Battery Park City

24 **25**

Cedar St

Pine St

Water St

DOWNTOWN

18

20 **21**

29 **30**

Wall St

Front St

FDR Drive

Rector St

Broadway

31

Pearl St

Exchange Pl

32

EAST RIVER

Beaver St

Broad St

33

34

35

Stone St

36

West St

Bridge St

Pearl St

Battery Pl

Whitehall St

State St

Battery Park

500 ft

START:
City Hall
(260 Broadway)

END:
Fraunces Tavern
(54 Pearl Street)

TOUR TIME:
About 3 hours

CHAPTERS:
1, 2, 5

City Hall

City Hall Park

The Woolworth Building

1. Start at the eastern side of New York's **City Hall**, completed in 1812. The building is a national historic landmark bounded by four curving streets: Broadway, Chambers Street, Park Row and Centre Street.

2. On the Centre Street side (the eastern side) of City Hall, notice the footpath that leads across the **Brooklyn Bridge**. After the American Revolution, New York City was America's capital. The first executive mansion, occupied by George Washington during his presidency, once stood right here but was demolished to build the Brooklyn Bridge ramp that now connects Manhattan to Brooklyn.

3. Walk south (downtown) as Centre Street curves around **City Hall Park**, the site of many celebrations and protests. Walk past the intersection of Spruce Street, where Centre Street becomes Park Row, for the best view of City Hall.

4. Across from City Hall at the corner of Park Row and Broadway is The Woolworth Building, one of the most successful examples of early high-rise construction. **The Woolworth Building** was the tallest building on earth when it opened in 1913 (the Chrysler Building surpassed it in 1930). Frequently illuminated at night, it's still renowned as one of the tallest buildings in New York.

5. Cross Broadway toward The Woolworth Building, then turn left (south) on Broadway. Continue walking straight ahead to **St. Paul's Chapel**, just south of Vesey Street, the oldest public building in continuous use in New York City. Built in 1766, it is the only colonial church still standing in Manhattan.

6. Turn right, and enter the chapel. President George Washington worshipped here on his Inauguration Day and during the years of his presidency. In 2001, St. Paul's Chapel served as a temporary refuge for heroic recovery workers digging through the rubble following the 9/11 disaster. Today, the interior is filled with artifacts from that demanding chapter. St. Paul's Chapel now overflows with warm wishes from around the world in memory of 9/11.

St. Paul's Chapel

7. After viewing the free exhibit, exit through the rear of St. Paul's Chapel, into its historic cemetery where some of America's first colonists from the 1700s are buried. When the Twin Towers collapsed, this graveyard was completely covered with several inches of ashes and dust.

Washington at St. Paul's, 1789

8. It's here that you'll encounter your first view of the new **One World Trade Center**, 1,776 feet high. This tour approaches the famous Freedom Tower through the 9/11 Memorial Park, the place that New Yorkers often call Ground Zero.

St. Paul's Chapel's cemetery

9. Follow the paths to the cemetery exit, then turn to the left (south) on Church Street.

10. Walk three short blocks down Church Street to Liberty Street.

One World Trade Center

11. At the corner of Liberty Street, turn right (west) to the **9/11 Memorial Park**. Admission is free. An explanatory brochure is available for free in nearby kiosks, published in eight languages.

12. Directly ahead, water cascades into two enormous **memorial pools** on the exact sites of the original Twin Towers. The names of all 2,983 victims who perished on September 11, 2001 are

9/11 Memorial Pool

Inscribed names of 9/11 victims

9/11 Memorial Museum

9/11 Memorial Park

Twin Towers

Zuccotti Park

inscribed in the parapet walls along the perimeter, including employees, visitors and passersby at the World Trade Center, plus the passengers and crew from the four planes that were commandeered and crashed into the World Trade Center, the Pentagon, and in Shanksville, Pennsylvania. These two one-acre pools are the largest man-made waterfalls in the U.S. (For an especially poignant photo, come back at dusk when the pools are illuminated.)

13. The entrance to the **9/11 Memorial Museum** stands to the east of the fountains. Same-day passes are usually available (at a variety of prices, including discounts for veterans, children and seniors), but tickets can be purchased online in advance at: www.911memorial.org. The museum is open daily from 9 a.m. to 8 p.m., and Fridays and Saturdays until 9 p.m. (Complimentary admission at all times for families of 9/11 victims. See online for details and reservations.)

14. Plan to spend about two hours in this large and powerful underground museum. Its exhibits explain the global significance of what happened here through artifacts and multimedia presentations. Docents are stationed throughout the museum to give details about the displays. The Education Center is recommended (at no extra cost) for families with pre-high school-age children; hands-on activities help young visitors understand what's on view.

15. After visiting the museum, walk back to Liberty Street and turn left (east), heading toward Broadway and the heart of the Financial District.

16. Optional: The small park on Liberty Street between Trinity Place and Broadway is a popular spot to relax and enjoy a quick lunch from many

licensed food vendors that surround the park.

17. Continue straight ahead (east) on Liberty Street, directly to Broadway.

18. At the corner of Liberty Street and Broadway, turn right (south). Steps down Broadway, is **Trinity Church**, New York's first Episcopal Church. King William III of England issued its original charter in 1697, but its colonial parishioners were more interested in severing their ties with England. Members of the First and Second Continental Congresses worshipped here. Alexander Hamilton, America's first Secretary of the Treasury, his wife Elizabeth Schuyler Hamilton, and one signer of the Declaration of Independence, Francis Lewis, are buried in the historic cemetery.

19. Trinity Church stands at the apex of Wall Street, named for the long wall that early Dutch settlers built here to keep out English colonists and to protect themselves from attacks by Native American tribes that populated Manhattan Island.

20. Turn to the left, cross Broadway, and stroll east on Wall Street. You'll pass a private entrance to the **New York Stock Exchange** (11 Wall Street, on the right). Continue straight ahead to the public square at the intersection of Wall Street and Broad Street for a better view of the NY Stock Exchange. This is one of the most famous intersections in American history, for . . .

21. Here is **Federal Hall**, America's original Capitol. You're standing where the first Americans stood as they witnessed the inauguration of America's first president: George Washington was inaugurated here in 1789. The Bill of Rights was signed into law here in 1791.

Trinity Church from Wall Street

Alexander Hamilton

New York Stock Exchange

Federal Hall

Washington's Inauguration, 1789

Washington's inaugural address

28 Liberty Plaza

Group of Four Trees

Federal Reserve

Federal Reserve scene in *Die Hard with a Vengeance*, 1995

22. Admission to Federal Hall is free. Among the displays inside is President Washington's handwritten inaugural address, which he delivered to the U.S. Senate on Inauguration Day.

23. To continue the tour, notice that on the western side of Federal Hall, Broad Street's name changes to Nassau Street. Walk north on Nassau Street, beside Federal Hall toward Pine Street.

24. Turn right (east) on Pine Street, along the back wall of Federal Hall.

25. At the corner of Pine Street and William Street, you'll see the very modern headquarters for the Chase Bank at **28 Liberty Plaza** (former One Chase Manhattan Plaza). The modern sculpture entitled **Group of Four Trees**, created by Jean Dubuffet, was commissioned, then gifted, by David Rockefeller in 1969 for the Bank.

26. Turn left (north) to enter 28 Liberty Plaza, then follow the plaza to the north and west, to the intersection of Nassau Street and Liberty Street.

27. The imposing building across the street that looks like a fortress on the corner of Liberty Street and Nassau Street is the **Federal Reserve**. This landmark building, built in 1924, houses the famous gold bars that back up America's currency, even more gold than Fort Knox. The stockpile rests in vaults five stories underground, safely embedded in Manhattan's solid bedrock.

28. Walk down the steps from the Plaza (or wheelchair ramp at Pine Street), then turn to the right (east) to walk along the front of the Federal Reserve. At the corner of William Street, turn right (south) to walk along the border of the Plaza.

29. The opulent towers erected on these narrow streets are bastions to finance, built by banks that no longer exist. At the corner of Wall Street, turn left (east).

Museum of American Finance

30. On the north side, 48 Wall Street once housed The Bank of New York, but is now the **Museum of American Finance**. Across the street, 55 Wall Street was the site of the original **Merchants' Exchange**, a forerunner to the NY Stock Exchange. It later became headquarters for Citibank (once known as First National City Bank). The bankers retained architect Stanford White to double the size of the building, adding its present façade of Corinthian columns. No longer a bank, this historic site is now full of restaurants and condominiums.

Original Merchants' Exchange

31. At the end of the block, turn right (south) onto Hanover Street. Walk one block to the corner of Exchange Place and turn right (west) to observe **20 Exchange Place**, a skyscraper from 1930. When National City Bank merged with Farmers Loan and Trust (the predecessor to Citigroup), this was the corporate headquarters. Still one of New York's tallest buildings, this commercial landmark is now converted into residences.

20 Exchange Place

32. Walk to the corner of Exchange Place and William Street, then turn left and keep walking south. At the next intersection, follow South William Street as it curves southwestward. During the city's first years, Dutch settlers occupied this side of Wall Street, the area they called **Nieuw Amsterdam**.

Exchange Place and William Street

33. Walk along picturesque South William Street to the corner of tiny Mill Lane. Turn left and walk through Mill Lane to the historic **Stone Street landmark district**, with its many outdoor dining tables that are serviced by the restaurants nearby.

Nieuw Amsterdam

Stone Street Landmark District

Stone Street

Fraunces Tavern

Fraunces Tavern, 1895

Washington's farewell, 1783

34. At Stone Street, turn to the right and follow the curving street, which is reputed to be the first New York City street that was paved (with cobblestones) by the Dutch circa 1658. Although the Dutch called it High Street, the British called it Duke Street, in honor of the Duke of York. After the American Revolution, there were no more honors for British dukes, and the place was renamed Stone Street in 1794. The early buildings were destroyed in a fire in 1835, replaced by these "counting houses" (as accounting offices were once called). The façades and sidewalks were restored in the 1990s.

35. Follow Stone Street to its end, where it intersects with Pearl Street. Then turn left (east) to walk for one final block along Pearl Street. Before New York Harbor was built, when tides lapped against the sandy beach nearby, this street was known as Mother-of-Pearl Street for the shiny shells that were frequently discovered here.

36. Stop at the corner of Pearl Street and Broad Street, the site of **Fraunces Tavern**, founded as the Queen's Head Tavern in 1762, and later run by Samuel Fraunces. At the end of the American Revolution, it was here on the second floor that General George Washington dismissed his commanders. The war with Britain was over; an independent nation was born. Not a moment for celebration, this was the site of Washington's famous and solemn farewell.

37. Fraunces Tavern is a national landmark but also a functioning restaurant, a great place to raise a glass and toast the sprawling history of New York, New York.

Brooklyn Bridge, 1899

Chinatown (Mott Street), 1906

The Bowery near Grand Street, c. 1900

CHINATOWN/SOHO

Since New York's first residents settled in the lower region of the island of Manhattan, this area's history is rich. Today, it's a vibrant display of many cultures, proving New York's moniker as "the great melting pot." This walk winds through four distinct neighborhoods.

START:
Information Kiosk at Baxter Street at Canal Street

END:
Washington Square

Tour Time:
About 2.5 hours

Chapters:
7, 19, 22, 23, 24

NYC information Kiosk

Columbus Park, 1905

Site of Five Points

1. Start at the Official **NYC Information Kiosk** at the intersection of Baxter Street and Canal Street.

2. Walk south (right) on Baxter Street until you arrive at **Columbus Park**, at the corner of Bayard Street. Continue walking along the park, until Baxter Street meets Worth Street; Cross Street (now Mosco Street) once met here as well. Before the Civil War, this was New York's worst slum (as depicted in Martin Scorsese's film *Gangs of New York*), an area called Five Points (for all these intersecting streets) populated primarily by Irish toughs.

3. There are no traces of **Five Points** any longer; those buildings were demolished, street patterns revised and Chinese settlers moved in when the Irish moved out. But use your imagination to picture Paradise Square and the infamous Old Brewery, long since buried under the New York State Supreme Court building at 60 Centre Street.

4. Walk east (left) to **Chatham Square**—also known as Kimlau Square—where Worth Street, Saint James Street, Park Row, and Mott Street all converge in one confusing intersection.

5. Follow Mott Street as it curves uptown (north), considered by many to be the "Main Street" of Manhattan's Chinatown. Most longtime residents are of Cantonese descent, but in later years a new dialect arrived from Hong Kong. Unlike the gentrified Chinatowns in other American cities, New York's Chinatown is a place for immigrants to get a new start. It's the rare place where you'll find Hong Kong, Vietnamese, Cantonese, Szechuan and Mandarin restaurants beside fish markets and herbalists, as well as contemporary fashions and art galleries.

6. Continue the stroll up **Mott Street** to Canal Street. Turn left (west) on Canal Street, a very busy shopping street.

7. Walk one block, to **Mulberry Street**. Turn right (north), crossing Canal Street to walk up Mulberry Street.

Chatham Square

8. Canal Street is the abrupt dividing line between Chinatown and the neighborhood known as Little Italy. Here you'll find blocks of Italian cultural attractions, from large restaurants to tiny espresso cafés and pastry shops.

Mott Street

9. Walk north on Mulberry Street through the streets of **Little Italy**. Although mafia characters in *The Godfather* and *The Sopranos* are pure fiction, their real-life counterparts, the Five Families that control organized crime, have historically called this neighborhood home. Mafia "rub-outs" are rare, but not uncommon, here.

10. For example, between Hester Street and Grand Street, you'll pass Umberto's Clam House. Shortly after Mafia don Joe Colombo was shot, Joey Gallo—the prime suspect in the Colombo shooting—was shot in gangland style at **Umbertos Clam House** in 1972. The restaurant relocated to 132 Mulberry Street, but hasn't shed its colorful reputation.

Little Italy

11. At the corner of Mulberry Street and Grand Street, consider a sweet diversion just a few paces to the right (east). **Ferrara Bakery and Café** (195 Grand Street) has been a neighborhood institution since 1892, providing pastries to some local restaurants as well as catering some opulent weddings. Stop in for a gelato or cannoli to enjoy as your stroll continues.

Umbertos Clam House

Ferrara Bakery and Café

Strolling Little Italy

Corner of Spring Street

Police Building

Spring Street

12. Take a moment to look up and down **Broome Street**. In the early 1960s, Robert Moses proposed a Lower Manhattan Expressway that would connect the Holland Tunnel with the Williamsburg and Manhattan bridges. The planned eight-lane highway would have displaced nearly 2,000 residents and destroyed historic buildings and businesses along fourteen blocks in SoHo and Little Italy. Thanks to the work of preservationists led by activist Jane Jacobs, the plan was defeated in 1964, and the neighborhood retains its historic charm.

13. Continue walking north on Mulberry Street. You'll soon notice a change in the neighborhood again, as you approach an area that real estate brokers call NoLIta (for North Of Little Italy). Continue on Mulberry Street to the corner of Spring Street.

14. Turn left (west) onto Spring Street, a busy shopping street on the edge of SoHo.

15. Stay on Spring Street, but look to your left, down Lafayette Street to view the ornate **Police Building**, built in 1909 as the NYPD headquarters. When the Police Department moved out in 1973, the building became a New York City landmark. Due to the city's chronic housing shortage, many large commercial buildings in this area have been converted to residential use including the Police Building, which became fifty-five spacious condominiums in 1988.

16. Continue walking west on Spring Street.

17. At the corner of Broadway, turn right (north) and stroll along busy Broadway for one block. These buildings were built for the garment industry and

light manufacturing, but today many of these floors are lofts where artists live and work instead.

18. Stop at the corner of Prince Street to note two famous buildings. **The Singer Sewing Machine Company** is a New York City landmark, built in 1902. (Singer promptly outgrew this place and built much larger headquarters on Liberty Street in 1908.) In the 1970s, this building became one of the first manufacturing buildings on Broadway to be converted into residential lofts. Shaped like an "L", you'll see more of the building around the corner on Prince Street.

The Singer Building

19. Stay on this corner to observe another kind of history. On the northwest corner of Broadway and Prince Street, the loft on the second floor of **565 Broadway** is the site of MTV's first season of *The Real World*, a program that many people consider the original reality television show. The building has undergone some renovations and the neighborhood is far more populous than it was in those 1992 broadcasts, but this is the place that launched hopes and heartbreaks, and many entertainment careers.

565 Broadway

SoHo scene, West Broadway

20. Cross Broadway, heading west on Prince Street. This area is a New York City landmark district, not for the unique interiors of artists' lofts above, but for the rare exterior facades made of cast-iron. The **SoHo-Cast Iron District** spans twenty-six city blocks and includes about 500 buildings.

Cast-iron building

21. At the corner of Greene Street, turn right (north) to see an entire block of cast-iron buildings on a cobblestone street. Fitting these large panels of cast-iron together to form an exterior facade enabled developers to erect buildings rapidly. Most buildings in the SoHo-Cast Iron District were built

Ghost (1990) showed SoHo life

Silver Towers

Picasso's *Bust of Sylvette*

Keith Haring

The Bitter End

Bob Dylan

in the decades shortly before and after the Civil War. The construction process fell out of favor with the invention of steel, an even stronger material that made New York's skyscrapers possible. No longer used for manufacturing, all of these buildings are now live/work lofts.

22. Keep walking north on Greene Street. SoHo officially ends at Houston Street.

23. From Greene Street, cross to the north side of Houston Street, heading toward some modern high-rise apartments known as the **Silver Towers**. This is faculty housing built by New York University, with a surprise in its center.

24. Turn left (west) and walk a short distance to the corner of Wooster Street, then turn right (north) to enter the apartment complex, which was designed by architect I.M. Pei.

25. In the center you'll discover a giant sculpture by Pablo Picasso. Entitled ***Bust of Sylvette***, it was a gift to New York University in 1968.

26. Walk past the sculpture then turn to the left (west) to exit.

27. Walking down the steps that lead from the university apartments, you'll be on LaGuardia Place, home of the late artist Keith Haring.

28. Turn to the right (north) and walk to the corner of Bleecker Street.

29. Turn left (west) and cross LaGuardia Place to explore Bleecker Street, the home of beatniks in the 1950s and early 1960s. Some of the beatniks' historic coffee houses still stand, although the

neighborhood has evolved around them.

30. At 147 Bleecker Street, you'll find **The Bitter End**, where an extraordinary list of performers got their starts, including Bob Dylan, Joan Baez, Billy Joel, Jackson Browne, Joni Mitchell, George Carlin, Judy Collins, Pete Seeger, James Taylor, and more.

San Remo on MacDougal St., 1950s

31. Keep walking west on Bleecker Street until you reach **MacDougal Street**; then turn right (north).

32. The coffee houses from the Beat Generation continue here, although many have evolved to suit new tastes over the decades. Walk north on MacDougal Street, past unique mom-and-pop shops for food and clothing.

Café Wha?

33. Near the middle of the block, stop at the intersecting street called Minetta Lane. At that corner, you'll find **Café Wha?**, another Beat Generation establishment with an astounding list of performers. Even older than The Bitter End, Café Wha was a regular hangout for poet Allen Ginsberg, a long-time resident of Greenwich Village. Performers who launched their careers here include: Bob Dylan, Jimi Hendrix, Bruce Springsteen, Kool and the Gang, and Peter, Paul & Mary, to name a few.

Café Reggio

34. Stay on MacDougal Street and continue walking north. At the corner of Washington Square, turn right (east). The brick building on this corner is the **law school for New York University**, the place where longtime New Yorker John F. Kennedy, Jr. famously earned his law degree.

NYU School of Law

35. Cross the street to enter **Washington Square Park**, the epicenter of Greenwich Village, and a colorful place to relax.

Washington Square Park

GREENWICH VILLAGE

Greenwich Village was once a bucolic suburb of New York City. Since then, artists, activists, beatniks and bohemians have all called it home. This tour starts at Washington Square Park, the center of it all, and explores the neighborhood's uniquely winding streets, built before the grid system was adopted.

CHELSEA

Ninth Ave

Eighth Ave

Seventh Ave

Union Sq

W 14th St

W 12th St

High Line

32

Gansevoort St

Greenwich Ave

31

Horatio St

Whitney Museum

Jane St

MEAT PACKING

Waverly Pl

W 10th St

Sixth Ave

Fifth Ave

30

W 12th St

Bethune St

W 4th St

Bank St

Bleecker St

24

23

22

W 11th St

26

5

4

2

1

Perry St

25

Washington Pl

Washington Square Park

29

21

7

W 4th St

Charles St

20

19

Jones St

W 3rd St

W 10th St

Christopher St

17

16

10

Grove St

GREENWICH VILLAGE

Thompson St

12

11

MacDougal St

Sullivan St

LaGuardia Pl

27

Bedford St

Houston St

Barrow St

Greenwich St

Hudson St

Prince St

Morton St

James J. Walker Park

Downing St

SoHo

Leroy St

Spring St

Clarkson St

W Houston St

Hudson River Greenway

King St

Broome St

Charlton St

Grand St

West St

Vandam St

HUDSON RIVER

Holland Tunnel

Canal St

1000 ft

START:
Washington Square Park

END:
The Highline

Tour Time:
About 3.5 hours

Chapters:
3, 4, 5, 20, 25

1. From the **Washington Square Arch**, facing Fifth Avenue, turn to the left and walk west. The street name of Washington Square North changes to Waverly Place (Note: Greenwich Village streets were determined before Manhattan's grid pattern was adopted, be prepared for circuitous streets that don't conform to true east and west. That's part of Greenwich Village's charm.)

2. Continue walking west on Waverly Place, past Sixth Avenue, also known as Avenue of the Americas.

3. Notice the curbstones at the sidewalk's edge on either side of Waverly Place. That stone doesn't exist anywhere else on this continent. These hewed curbstones originally served as ballast in the hulls of English ships heading to New York, then a British colony. You'll see these non-indigenous gray curbstones throughout almost all streets in Greenwich Village west of Sixth Avenue.

Washington Square Arch

4. Turn to the right (north). Cross the intersection of Waverly Place and Christopher Street near the triangular Christopher Park, then walk to 53 Christopher Street. A famous Civil Rights protest occurred at this bar in June 1969, when New York City policemen arrived at midnight at the **Stonewall Inn** to harass its gay patrons and shake down the management for graft. It was an all-too-common occurrence, but this time a bottle went flying as gays, trans, and lesbians fought back against the police. The melee continued for three days, as more gays from around the Village battled against the cops indoors and around the park across the street. Gay people everywhere acknowledge the Stonewall Rebellion as the beginning of the international gay rights movement. The Stonewall Inn was destroyed

Stonewall Inn

(though it's reopened under new management, bearing little resemblance to the original).

5. Walk west to the corner of Christopher Street, then turn left and cross the street onto the triangular park. Enter the park from its Seventh Avenue side. **A sculpture of two gay couples**, created by sculptor George Segal, quietly commemorates the famous protest of 1969 and its loving aftermath.

Sculpture by George Segal

Marie's Crisis Café

6. Exiting the park, walk a few paces south to return to Waverly Place. Cross Seventh Avenue, where the street's name changes to Grove Street.

7. At 59 Grove Street, you'll find **Marie's Crisis Café**. A tavern since colonial days, patronized by Thomas Paine and other colonial patriots, it's been operating at this location ever since.

Thomas Paine

8. Continue walking west on Grove Street, noting the ironwork in front of these houses. Since they were built before roads were paved, you'll see an occasional shoe scraper built into the original ironwork near the lower steps on these stoops. You're viewing some of the oldest houses still standing in America.

Houses on Grove Street

9. Grove Street is a typical tree-lined street in Greenwich Village. Streets like this one extend to the north and south; they've provided homes for generations of notable Americans, including playwright Eugene O'Neill, activists John Reed, Louise Bryant and Emma Goldman, actors Bette Midler, Sarah Jessica Parker and Matthew Broderick, and many, many more.

Shoe scraper

10. Continue walking on Grove Street to the corner of Bedford Street, then turn left (south).

75 1/2 Bedford Street

Cherry Lane Theatre

Godspell poster

Wooden house

102 Bedford Street

11. A few paces from the corner of Bedford Street and Commerce Street, you'll see the smallest house in New York at **75 1/2 Bedford Street**. Once the home of poet Edna St. Vincent Millay, the tiny house is just ten feet wide; it sold in 2010 for just over $2 million.

12. From Bedford Street, turn west onto Commerce Street. It's the site of the **Cherry Lane Theatre**, off-Broadway's first theater, founded by Edna St. Vincent Millay and friends in 1924. It's the home of many theatrical successes, including the original productions of *Godspell*; *Nunsense*; *True West*; *To Be Young, Gifted and Black*; *Little Mary Sunshine*; and many more.

13. Follow the curve of Commerce Street to where it intersects again with Barrow Street. Turn right (east) onto Barrow Street, back to Bedford Street. At the corner of Bedford Street, turn left (north) and walk for one block to the corner of Grove Street.

14. On the northeast corner of Bedford Street and Grove Street stands one of the last remaining wooden houses in all of New York City.

15. The Tudor house next door at **102 Bedford Street** has been home to several famous actors, including Errol Flynn and Charles Laughton.

16. Turn left (west) onto Grove Street. Halfway down the block, the street curves. On the south side of the street, look for the wrought-iron gate that permits a peek at **Grove Court**, a collection of tiny private houses with a common garden in front, one of Greenwich Village's most charming and historic addresses.

17. Continue walking down Grove Street to Hudson

Street. When Vice President John Adams lived in Greenwich Village, the Hudson River actually lapped against the shore here, but as the city's hills were flattened, landfill was added to make way for additional streets to the west. Directly ahead, on that landfill on the western side of Hudson Street stands **The Church of St. Luke in the Fields**.

Grove Court

18. Since Greenwich Village's population grew as residents from the congested area near today's Financial District relocated here, the churches relocated, too. St. Luke's Church was built as an extension of the Trinity Church parish further downtown. Its tiny Meditation Garden is often open to the public. Enter from Hudson Street.

St. Luke in the Fields Church

19. Turn right and walk north on Hudson Street to Christopher Street, one of the major shopping streets of Greenwich Village. Turn right (east) onto Christopher Street, where you'll pass the **Lucille Lortel Theatre**. Known for decades as the Theatre de Lys, it proved the viability of off-Broadway by presenting *The Threepenny Opera* (which ran for seven years!) with Lotte Lenya, John Astin, Paul Dooley, and the very young Beatrice Arthur among its original cast. This theater launched many shows that moved to larger quarters uptown on Broadway.

Lucille Lortel Theatre

20. Continue to walk east on Christopher Street, where you'll find many quaint shops, including **McNulty's Tea and Coffee Co.**, at 109 Christopher Street, a Village institution since 1895.

McNulty's Tea and Coffee Co.

21. Walk to the corner of Bleecker Street, then turn left to view more scenic streets of Greenwich Village. Notice that the street signs are color-coded. Blocks with historic significance have brown signs; blocks not protected by landmark status have green street signs.

Color-coded street signs

74 Charles Street

Perry Street

White Horse Tavern

Dylan Thomas at the White Horse

Condominiums on Hudson River

22. Walk north for two blocks on Bleecker Street, then turn right (east) onto Charles Street to observe the residential architecture. The heavy cornices at the tops of these buildings are made of cast-iron to protect the buildings from inclement weather at the vulnerable junction where the flat roof meets the front facade. The building at **74 Charles Street** was the New York home of songwriter Woody Guthrie. Author Sinclair Lewis lived across the street, at **69 Charles Street**.

23. At the corner of West 4th Street, turn left (north) and walk one block to the corner of Perry Street.

24. Turn left (west) onto **Perry Street** to savor the diverse architecture of Greenwich Village, from apartment buildings to elegant one-family houses; they all comprise one of America's largest landmark districts.

25. On Perry Street, cross Hudson Street, then turn right (north) and walk along the west side of Hudson Street. You'll soon encounter **The White Horse Tavern**, one of the oldest pubs in America, a place frequented by Welsh author and poet Dylan Thomas. He set a record here, downing eighteen whiskies in one night—then died the next morning.

26. At the corner of West 11th Street, turn left (west) and walk to the Hudson River. Cross Washington Street, the cusp of the landmark district. The buildings between here and the Hudson River are newly constructed condominiums or converted warehouses from the era when freighters lined the (now-demolished) piers along the river. Some of the residents in this modern area include actors Harrison Ford, Calista Flockhart and Nicole Kidman; the buildings are designed by some of

the world's most celebrated architects, including Richard Meier and Frank Gehry.

27. Cross West Street to enter Henry Hudson Park. It's a great place for people-watching, relaxing, a snack, or a stroll along the Hudson River in either direction.

28. Then, turn around and walk back (east) to Washington Street.

29. At Washington Street, turn left (north) to visit more history.

30. Greenwich Village ends where the **Meatpacking District** begins, just north of West 12th Street. It's where butchers once packaged freshly slaughtered meats, where animal blood was not an uncommon sight on the cobblestone streets. Today the neighborhood is a vibrant collection of boutiques and restaurants (as frequently seen in reruns of HBO's *Sex and the City*).

31. At Washington Street and Gansevoort Street, climb the stairs (or take the elevator) to a unique Manhattan getaway called **The High Line.** Elevated trains once ran here, transporting goods from the piers, warehouses, and the Meatpacking District to vendors across America. In 2015 the **Whitney Museum of American Art**, a six-story, Renzo Piano-designed modern building, arrived at 99 Gansevoort Street as an anchor of the High Line.

32. Today, the High Line is a landscaped promenade. Relax along the Hudson River to the west, strolling above the traffic, where you can observe historic Chelsea to the east.

Meatpacking District

The High Line and Whitney Museum

The High Line

Whitney Museum

The High Line in Chelsea

ASTOR PLACE

Astor Place takes its name from one of the most powerful families in New York history. This tour explores the area's artistic legacy—from the elegant townhouses straight out of Henry James' Washington Square to the studios of the Ashcan School and today's Public Theater.

START:
Washington Square Park

END:
Astor Library

TOUR TIME:
About 1.5 hours

CHAPTERS:
5, 6, 10, 17

Fountain in Washington Square

Marble arch by Stanford White

Washington Square North

1. Start at the fountain in **Washington Square**. Before plumbing was installed under Greenwich Village streets, this was the site of the communal well where Village residents pumped their water.

2. In New York's earliest years, this park was a potter's field, a mass burial ground for indigent New Yorkers and those who died of cholera. There are thousands of unmarked graves beneath these paving stones in Washington Square.

3. The marble arch featuring General George Washington was designed by renowned architect Stanford White and built in 1892; it marks the beginning of Fifth Avenue.

4. All along the northern end of the park, **Washington Square North** is lined with some of the earliest luxury residences in America. Although they originally lacked indoor plumbing, these townhouses were built as homes for some of New York's wealthiest families. Henry James' famous novel *Washington Square* imagines life in these elegant homes; it's the source material for both the award-winning play and movie *The Heiress*. Henry James lived and worked from One Washington Square North; novelist Edith Wharton lived at No. 7. Today, most of these buildings are used as offices for New York University.

5. At the northwest corner of the park, turn right and cross Washington Square North, heading uptown on MacDougal Street.

6. Halfway up the block on the right (east) side, you'll find **MacDougal Alley**. These small buildings once housed the carriages owned by the residents of the townhouses on Washington Square North. Decades later, they gained fame when Gertrude

Vanderbilt Whitney and other artists gentrified these empty buildings into art studios, which art critics dubbed "the Ashcan School." Some of the artists who joined Mrs. Whitney included: Robert Henri, George Bellows, William Glackens, George Luks, Everett Shinn, and John Sloan. Attracted by the art scene, Jackson Pollock moved into 9 MacDougal Alley in 1949.

MacDougal Alley

7. Continue walking north on MacDougal Street, then turn right onto Eighth Street and walk east. You'll pass **8 West 8th Street**, a building acquired by Gertrude Vanderbilt Whitney and the Ashcan artists as a place to display their art. It's the original site of the Whitney Museum of American Art.

8 West 8th Street

8. Cross Fifth Avenue at the corner of 8th Street and turn right (south) past the One Fifth Avenue apartment house. Halfway down the block you'll discover the **Washington Mews**, two rows of carriage houses formerly owned by the residents on Washington Square. Notice the original Belgian blocks that pave this street. All of Greenwich Village was once paved with these brick-shaped stones.

Gertrude V. Whitney by Robert Henri

9. Walk all the way through the Washington Mews and you'll emerge on the campus of **New York University**, the largest private educational institution in the U.S., and one of the largest owners of real estate in New York City. Turn right, heading south toward Washington Square East.

Washington Mews

10. At the corner of Washington Place, turn left and walk further east, through the New York University campus, to the corner of Greene Street.

11. The **Triangle Shirtwaist Company** once occupied the top three floors at this northwest

Site of Triangle Shirtwaist Company

249

Broadway buildings

Grace Church

Astor Place

Ukrainian Festival in East Village

The Cooper Union

corner. In 1911, a spark from a primitive electric sewing machine ignited a fire. Women laborers, locked in the building while working, jumped from the windows to their deaths as the fire raged out of control. The tragic scene led to new fire-safety laws, workers rights, and the creation of the International Ladies' Garment Workers' Union.

12. Continue walking east on Washington Place; then turn left on Broadway, heading uptown. These Broadway buildings were the sites of many garment-related industries, with a showroom on the ground floor and sweatshops upstairs. Today, some of these buildings have been converted into residential lofts, while others are still used for offices and light manufacturing.

13. On Broadway at 10th Street, you'll find **Grace Church**, the first construction project by architect James Renwick, who gained greater fame as the architect for St. Patrick's Cathedral. Prior to this church's construction, the site was a grove of trees maintained by owner Hendrick Brevoort, who guarded the site with a live bear.

14. Turn right on 10th Street and walk east. At Lafayette Street, turn right and walk to **Astor Place**. For most of the twentieth century, this area was home to people of Eastern-European ancestry.

15. **The Cooper Union** (the brown building on Astor Place) is one of America's oldest and most prestigious colleges for art, architecture and engineering. Tuition is free and competition for acceptance is fierce, with less than five percent of applicants awarded acceptance. Abraham Lincoln debated Stephen Douglas in the Great Hall at Cooper Union, which led to his nomination for president. Subsequent presidents to speak in the

Great Hall include Ulysses S. Grant, William Taft, Theodore Roosevelt, Woodrow Wilson, Bill Clinton, and Barack Obama.

St. Mark's Place

16. Cross Third Avenue as you continue walking east. Astor Place and Cooper Square become **St. Marks Place**, famous in the 1960s as the place for New York's hippie community to congregate. Gentrification has turned this into a multi-cultural neighborhood today, with many NYU students as residents as well.

St. Marks Place

17. Continue to the end of the block, then turn right onto Second Avenue, walk one block south, then turn right again, onto 7th Street.

Second Avenue

18. At 15 East 7th Street, you'll find **McSorley's Old Ale House**, the last of New York's "men only" pubs, until it was "liberated" by Gloria Steinem, an action successfully defended in court by the National Organization for Women in 1970. Today, McSorley's welcomes men and women patrons.

McSorley's Old Ale House

19. Walking west, you'll pass **Surma**, a fascinating Ukrainian shop that has imported and sold handmade Eastern-European artifacts since the early twentieth century.

20. Continuing to the west, you'll pass the modern **School of Architecture at the Cooper Union**. The triangular park between the old and new buildings at Cooper Union was the site of riots protesting the government's Civil War draft.

Surma

21. Continue west, crossing Cooper Square Park, then turn right on Fourth Avenue, heading again toward Astor Place. At the corner, turn left (west) and walk to Lafayette Street, then turn left again to walk down Lafayette Street.

School of Architecture

436-440 Lafayette Street

Colonnade Row

Colonnade Row, 1831

Astor Library (The Public Theater)

22. Observe the buildings across Lafayette Street. The building at **436-440 Lafayette Street** has a facade completely constructed of cast-iron. This precedent-setting process enabled builders to construct New York's large buildings more rapidly, and at a lower cost than assembling bricks and mortar.

23. Further down the block, notice the buildings with tall Greek columns. Built by John Jacob Astor as a much larger row of attached, opulent one-family townhouses, including one for oldest son William B. Astor and family, identical buildings once occupied most of the block, known as **Colonnade Row**. Over the decades many of these townhouses were demolished; the remaining facades are now local landmarks, a reminder of what is lost when neighborhoods evolve through new construction.

24. Across the street stands the former home of the **Astor Library**, built by John Jacob Astor to house his book collection. (It was later merged with books from James Lenox and Samuel Tilden to become the New York Public Library at Fifth Avenue and 42nd Street.) Before Astor constructed this redbrick library, this was the site of the 1,800-seat **Astor Place Opera House**, which was destroyed when "patriotic" Americans protested the appearance of a British performer soon after the War of 1812. Today the Astor Library has been reconfigured into **The Public Theater**. Some of Broadway's greatest successes began here, including the original productions of *Hair, Hamilton,* and *A Chorus Line*, a terrific example of how old construction can adapt to modern use.

Jefferson Market Courthouse, 1928

Westbeth Artists' Housing, 1930s

Madison Square Park, c. 1900

GRAMERCY PARK

Gramercy Park is the only private park in Manhattan.
Though only key-holders may enter, the charming
townhouses and tree-lined streets that surround it make up
one of the most beautiful sights in Manhattan.

Empire State
Building

E 34th St

Sixth Ave

Broadway

Fifth Ave

Madison Ave

E 30th St

E 28th St

Park Ave S

Lexington Ave

Third Ave

Second Ave

First Ave

Madison
Sq Park

W 23rd St

E 23rd St

FLATIRON

Gramercy
Park

W 20th St

E 20th St

GRAMERCY
PARK

W 17th St

E 17th St

Stuyvesant
Square

Union
Square

Irving Pl

W 14th St

E 14th St

Sixth Ave

Fifth Ave

University Pl

Broadway

Fourth Ave

Third Ave

Second Ave

First Ave

W 12th St

W 10th St

Greenwich Ave

E 9th St

E 8th St

Stuyvesant St

St. Marks Pl

Waverly Pl

Astor Pl

E 7th St

EAST
VILLAGE

Washington Sq N

Waverly Pl

Lafayette St

Washington Square Park

Washington Pl

Washington Pl

START:
Madison Square Park

END:
Union Square

TOUR TIME:
About 1.5 hours

CHAPTERS:
8, 14, 16

1. Broadway intersects Fifth Avenue at 23rd Street, creating an unusual triangle where one of the world's first skyscrapers, the **Flatiron Building**, was constructed. New Yorkers feared that it would be toppled by the wind, but its unseen superstructure of steel beneath the stone facade proved the durability of high-rise architecture instead.

2. The Flatiron's unusual shape caused winds to swirl toward **Madison Square Park**, frequently causing ladies' skirts to rise. Awaiting the glimpse of an ankle, young men often lined East 23rd Street at Madison Square Park until police officers gave them the "23-skidoo."

3. This location is also notable for the office buildings facing into Madison Square Park. Renowned architect Stanford White maintained his office here.

Flatiron Building

4. On Broadway, walk south (downtown) past the Flatiron Building (also known as 175 Fifth Avenue). The buildings from East 14th Street to East 23rd Street were known as **Ladies' Mile** for the fine fashions and millinery shops located here. These streets were once a fashion parade.

Madison Square Park

5. The cast-iron building at the corner of Broadway and East 20th Street (909 Broadway) is the former location of the **Lord & Taylor department store**. Turn left at this corner, heading east. (East 20th Street is also labeled Theodore Roosevelt Way.)

909 Broadway and Ladies' Mile

6. The brownstone at **28 East 20th Street** was the childhood home of President Theodore Roosevelt, who was born in 1858 and lived here for the first fifteen years of his life. Maintained by the National Park Service, this National Historic Landmark is open for tours Tuesday through Saturday.

7. Continue walking east. Upon crossing Park Avenue South, you'll enter the Gramercy Park Historic District, named for the landscaped park directly ahead.

Theodore Roosevelt birthplace

8. **Gramercy Park** is New York's only private park, just two blocks wide and one block long. Residents in the buildings surrounding the park are its sole key-holders, adding extra value to these exclusive addresses. Continue to walk east along this southern perimeter of the private park.

Gramercy Park

9. On the right, you'll discover the **National Arts Club**, built by Samuel Tilden (later a presidential candidate) and remodeled into a club by Calvert Vaux, the designer of Central Park. (The interiors of the club can be seen in Martin Scorsese's film *The Age of Innocence* starring Daniel Day-Lewis and Winona Ryder.) Past members have included artists Frederick Remington and Robert Henri, and presidents Theodore Roosevelt and Woodrow Wilson.

National Arts Club and Players Club

10. Next door at 16 Gramercy Park South is the **The Players Club**, another National Historic Landmark; its interior is only open to club members. Founded by Edwin Booth and Mark Twain, among others, it is the foremost gathering place for America's stage actors. Some current members include: Edie Falco, Ethan Hawke, Timothy Hutton, Al Pacino, Carol Burnett, Mary Tyler Moore; the list goes on.

The Age of Innocence, 1993

11. Turn to the left (north) to view Gramercy Park East. The building at the corner, **34 Gramercy Park**, is the first cooperative apartment building in New York. (Unlike today's condominiums, co-op owners buy shares in the building, much like joining a country club. Technically, selling a co-op apartment means selling those shares in the

The Players Club

34 Gramercy Park

Stanford White house

No. 3 and 4 Gramercy Park

James Harper

Pete's Tavern

building corporation.) James Cagney owned an apartment here, as did Margaret Hamilton, and John Carradine.

12. Walk to the corner of Gramercy Park East, then turn left (west) to stroll along Gramercy Park North. Near its center, notice the large gate where key-holding residents enter the park. Lexington Avenue begins here too, the street in the center that heads north. Julia Roberts, Victor Herbert, John Steinbeck, Thomas Edison, John Barrymore and Stanford White are just some of the many acclaimed individuals past and present who owned a key to this private park.

13. At the corner of the park, turn left (south) to view Gramercy Park West.

14. The building at **3 Gramercy Park West** was the final home for actor John Garfield, starring in a revival of *Golden Boy* on Broadway when he died. **No. 4 Gramercy Park** was the home of James Harper, publisher of *Harper's Magazine*, which featured stories by local authors such as Herman Melville, Mark Twain, and Horace Greeley. (His publishing company Harper & Row, today's Harper-Collins, has given us works by Tom Wolfe and Jonathan Franzen among many others.) Harper was elected Mayor of New York in 1844.

15. Turn left (east) at the corner of Gramercy Park South, and stroll past the The Players Club toward the intersecting street near the center of the park.

16. That intersecting street is Irving Place, named for renowned New York writer Washington Irving. Turn right (south) to stroll down Irving Place.

17. At the corner of Irving Place and East 18th Street, you'll find **Pete's Tavern**, one of the oldest continuously functioning bars in Manhattan, established in 1864. It was immortalized by writer, local resident and frequent patron O. Henry (a resident at 55 Irving Place), who drank himself to death (caused by cirrhosis of the liver) in the days before Prohibition.

Townhouses on 18th Street

18. For an architectural treat, turn left (east) on East 18th Street. While most Manhattan townhouses feature tall stoops with many stairs (like those along Gramercy Park West), the entrances to these landmark townhouses feature an "English basement," just a few steps up to the front door and a few steps down for the servant's entrance below. These are some of the oldest houses still standing in New York.

49 Irving Place

19. Turn around and return to Irving Place, crossing to the west side of the street, then turn left (south) to continue the downtown walk.

Washington Irving plaque

20. At the corner of East 17th Street, the building at **49 Irving Place** (also known as 122 East 17th Street) was the home of Washington Irving, author of *The Legend of Sleepy Hollow* among other titles; it was Irving who coined the term "Gotham" to refer to New York City. He also served as the first chairman of the Astor Library.

Union Square market

21. Turn right to walk west on East 17th Street. Directly ahead you'll see **Union Square**, the site of the first Labor Day celebration on September 5, 1882. It's been a center of political activism ever since: the place where Emma Goldman and generations of rabble-rousers have led protests and marches in their fight for human rights.

Union Square

TURTLE BAY

Once a marshy farmland, Turtle Bay has become home to movie stars and ambassadors alike. This tour starts in the international territory of the United Nations Headquarters, and ends at Riverview Terrace, one of Manhattan's most exclusive addresses.

UPPER EAST SIDE

E 63rd St

The Rockefeller
University

York Ave

Queensboro Bridge

E 58th St

E 57th St

MIDTOWN EAST

E 54th St

E 52nd St

Park Ave

Third Ave

Second Ave

First Ave

Sutton Pl S

Roosevelt
Island

26

25

23 24

22

20 21

18 19

17

14

13

12 11

9

E 49th St 6   7

E 48th St

5

4

3   2

E 45th St   1   United
Nations

Grand Central
Terminal

TURTLE BAY

EAST
RIVER

E 42nd St

Lexington Ave

First Ave

FDR Drive

Midtown Tunnel

MURRAY HILL

START:
United Nations

END:
Sutton Square

TOUR TIME:
About 2.5 hours

CHAPTERS:
9, 26

United Nations

Trump World Tower

Dag Hammarskjold Plaza

1. From the **United Nations**, cross First Avenue to its western side.

2. Walk north up First Avenue following the direction of the traffic to 47th Street. On the right, on First Avenue spanning 47th to 48th streets is **Trump World Tower**. When constructed, it was the tallest residential building in Manhattan.

3. Walk west on East 47th Street, also known as **Dag Hammarskjold Plaza**, the site of many demonstrations for human rights.

4. At Second Avenue, turn right. Walk north (uptown) one block. Take a left on 48th Street.

5. These are the historic **Turtle Bay Gardens townhouses**, all linked by an elegant common garden in back. Author E. B. White lived at **229 East 48th Street** while writing *Charlotte's Web*. Walk around this block by heading west, then north on Third Avenue; then view the other side of the complex from 49th Street, heading back to the east. Residents of these townhouses have included Katharine Hepburn (**244 East 49th Street**), Oscar-winning writer/director Garson Kanin with his actress wife Ruth Gordon (**242 East 49th Street**) composer Stephen Sondheim, and *Time* magazine publisher Henry Luce (**234 East 49th Street**).

6. Continue walking east on 49th Street to First Avenue.

7. Across First Avenue is **UN Plaza**, mixed-use condominium apartments. The building at 780 UN Plaza was once home to Johnny Carson and Truman Capote, among others.

8. Cross First Avenue at 49th Street; then follow the upper ramp onto Mitchell Place. Walk one block further east toward the East River and Beekman Place.

Turtle Bay Gardens townhouses

9. At the corner, you'll face **One Beekman Place**, the former home of John D. Rockefeller III. More notoriously, it was also the home to Mame Dennis, known as Auntie Mame in the famous book by her nephew, author Patrick Dennis, and in vivid incarnations on stage and in film. Mame's penthouse was later owned by the equally flamboyant Huntington Hartford, heir to a grocery-store fortune.

Katharine Hepburn

10. Continue to walk north to East 50th Street.

11. The red brick building at the corner of 50th Street (**17 Beekman Place**) was the one-family home of composer Irving Berlin, who lived in the house for the final four decades of his life. It's now the Consulate General of Luxembourg.

One Beekman Place

12. Turn left and stroll across and back on 50th Street. These elegant townhouses have been the homes to Oscar-nominee Dame Judith Anderson (**414 East 50th Street**), Oscar-nominee Julie Harris (**415 East 50th Street**), and architect Max Abramovitz (**419 East 50th Street**), whose prominent works include the headquarters for the United Nations and Avery Fisher Hall at Lincoln Center.

17 Beekman Place

13. Return to Beekman Place and observe the row of townhouses along its eastern side. While most buildings are now consulates for foreign governments, these former one-family residences have been the homes of architect Paul Rudolph (23 Beekman Place), award-winning author William

Irving Berlin

39 Beekman Place

Jacqueline and Aristotle Onassis

Apartment houses of Beekman Pl.

Dead End, 1937

Roosevelt Island

Shirer (**25-27 Beekman Place**), Broadway producer Billy Rose (**29 Beekman Place**), and Ashraf Pahlavi, the sister of the Shah of Iran (**33 Beekman Place**). Perhaps most notably, Aristotle Onassis purchased the house at the corner of East 51st Street (**39 Beekman Place**) as a gift for his new bride Jacqueline Kennedy Onassis. The paparazzi promptly set up a full-time vigil outside the house. Observing the lack of privacy, the Onassises never moved in.

14. At the corner of 51st Street, turn right and walk down the stairs and across the footbridge that leads to the East River. At the end of the bridge, you'll see grand apartment houses. Before these buildings were erected, this was a neighborhood in decline, the subject of the play and movie *Dead End* starring Humphrey Bogart and introducing The Dead End Kids, who went on to appear in a succession of films as the *Bowery Boys*.

15. On the other side of the East River is **Roosevelt Island**, a large complex of apartments accessible from Manhattan by a tram suspended on cables over the East River. Beyond it, the neon Silvercup sign advertises the site of a former commercial bakery that now serves as the Silvercup Studios, used for many film and television productions.

16. Facing downtown, you'll see a terrific view of the United Nations and the Williamsburg Bridge.

17. Return to Beekman Place; then walk west toward First Avenue. Stroll up First Avenue; then turn right onto 52nd Street. Note the Dead End sign. This was once the squalid home of the real-life Dead End Kids portrayed in films and on Broadway.

18. Two important buildings overlook the water. **River House** at 435 East 52nd Street has been the home to former Secretary of State Henry Kissinger, stage and film director Joshua Logan, *Time* magazine publisher Henry Luce and his playwright wife Clare Boothe Luce; also Marshall Field, Cornelius Vanderbilt Whitney, and Angier Biddle Duke.

Dead End sign at East 52nd St.

19. Across the street, **450 East 52nd Street** was the home of singer Bobby Short, British playwright and actor Noël Coward, and Broadway's leading lady Mary Martin. Most notably, Greta Garbo, the film star who "wanted to be alone," found her solace here for the last half of her life.

River House

20. Return to First Avenue and walk up to 54th Street, then turn right.

21. Note the large condominium halfway down the block, **River Tower**. One of its very first residents was the "Iron Butterfly" Imelda Marcos, wife of the deposed Philippine dictator, who reportedly arrived with over 400 pairs of shoes.

450 East 52nd Street (left)

22. Continue east to the corner of **Sutton Place South**; then turn left, heading uptown on Sutton Place South. The building at **36 Sutton Place South** (between 55th and 56th streets) was the home of Joan Crawford during the 1950s.

Greta Garbo in *Grand Hotel*, 1932

23. Sutton Place is one of New York's most exclusive addresses. Liza Minnelli, the record-setting performer who won an Oscar, a Grammy, an Emmy, and a Tony Award in one season lives around the corner on East 57th Street, and actress Helen Hayes made her home at **444 East 57th Street**. Stage and film star Lillian Gish called **430 East 57th Street** home for decades. Perhaps most

Sutton Place South

444 East 57th Street

Marilyn Monroe and Arthur Miller

One Sutton Place

Bridge from Riverview Terrace

notably, Marilyn Monroe and Arthur Miller lived on the 13th floor of 444 East 57th Street.

24. Feelin' groovy? Walk east to the small park overlooking the river, where you'll have a great photo op of the 59th Street Bridge (officially the **Ed Koch Queensboro Bridge**) made famous by Simon and Garfunkel in their "59th Street Bridge Song" and renamed for three-term mayor Ed Koch. If you time it right, you might even catch a photo of the Roosevelt Island tram in mid-air.

25. Walk up Sutton Place toward 58th Street. This row of townhouses along the east side has been owned by a number of illustrious residents. **One Sutton Place** has been home to oil baron J. Paul Getty, and later to H. J. Heinz II of Heinz Ketchup fame. **Two Sutton Place** was the home of entertainer George Jessel, and later, playwright William Saroyan.

26. At 58th Street, notice that the name changes to Sutton Square. Walk east toward the river and you'll find one of New York's most private cul-de-sacs, called **Riverview Terrace**.

George Bellows's New York

Born and raised in Columbus, Ohio, George Bellows attended Ohio State University, with the hope of becoming a professional baseball player. In 1904, before graduating, Bellows moved to New York City to study art with Robert Henri, where he found rich subject matter in the lives of the people in the booming metropolis, New York.

Men of the Docks, 1912, The National Gallery, London
Together with some draft horses, day laborers await jobs on the docks of Brooklyn on a winter morning.

Cliff Dwellers, 1913, Los Angeles County Museum of Art
On a hot summer day people spill out of tenement buildings into the streets of the Lower East Side between the Bowery and Catherine Slip below Chatham Square.

Stag at Sharkey's, 1909, The Cleveland Museum of Art
Bellows depicts a prize fight at Tom Sharkey's Athletic Club, a popular bar that was located directly across Broadway from his studio on 66th Street.

New York, 1911, National Gallery of Art
Bellows captures the tumult of a busy intersection in winter. Although the painting's general location is Madison Square at Broadway and 23rd Street, he imaginatively combined elements that could not be seen from a single viewpoint.

MIDTOWN

Midtown Manhattan is home to many of the great modern icons of New York City, including the New York Public Library, Rockefeller Center, and the Chrysler Building. A stroll through the area reveals traces of the many entrepreneurs who have shaped Manhattan, from Commodore Vanderbilt to Donald Trump.

CENTRAL PARK

Central Park
Zoo

UPPER EAST
SIDE

E 61st St

Columbus
Circle

W 57th St
Carnegie
Hall

E 57th St

Seventh Ave

Ave of the Americas

Fifth Ave

Madison Ave

Park Ave

Lexington Ave

Third Ave

Eighth Ave

Broadway

MIDTOWN

MoMA

W 52nd St

20

19

21

W 50th St

17

22

25

Saint
Bartholomew's

24

Waldorf-
Astoria Hotel

W 49th St

Rockefeller
Plaza

14

15

13

W 47th St

12

Times Square

11

10

E 45th St

Grand Central
Terminal

1

4

7

6

5

E 42nd St

Bryant
Park

NY
Public
Library

8

Broadway

E 37th St

The
Morgan
Library &
Museum

MURRAY HILL

Herald Square

START:
Grand Central Terminal

END:
Saint Bartholomew's
Church

TOUR TIME:
About 2 hours

CHAPTERS:
11, 12, 20, 26

Grand Central Terminal

GCT and the Chrysler Building

Commodore Hotel

1. Start in **Grand Central Terminal**, at the information desk marked by an opulent brass clock; its faces are opalescent glass. Cornelius Vanderbilt purchased the land here in 1869 for use as a train depot and rail yard. The current Beaux-Arts building—designed by two firms, Warren and Wetmore, and Reed and Stem—opened in 1913. To this day it is one of the world's busiest train stations, serving over 750,000 passengers a day.

2. Look up inside the Main Concourse. The ceiling is painted with a mural of the zodiac designed by French artist Paul César Helleu. If the vision of the sky looks unfamiliar, that's because it's painted backwards. The mural was restored as part of a program that began in 1996.

3. Exit the station via the corner of East 42nd Street and Lexington Avenue exit.

4. The **Chrysler Building** is located directly across the street. The Art Deco building was completed in 1930, and was then the tallest building in the world for just eleven months, until the completion of the Empire State Building.

5. Turn right (west) on 42nd Street. Here you will pass the Grand Hyatt New York, originally called **The Commodore Hotel** when it was built in 1919. Sixty years later, Donald Trump purchased the dilapidated property for a mere $10 million. Here "The Donald" created his signature look of mirrored finishes and polished stainless steel. The hotel was a key moment in the revitalization of Midtown, and in establishing Trump as a major force in New York real estate.

6. Continue walking west on East 42nd Street, past Grand Central Terminal on your right.

7. Continue walking west until you reach Fifth Avenue. Here, on your left (south), you will see the **New York Public Library**, designed by Carrère and Hastings, a little-known firm at the time. The cornerstone was laid in 1902 and construction was completed in 1911. The project cost $9 million (the equivalent of well over $200 million today).

The New York Public Library

8. In front of the library sit two famous lions—originally called Leo Astor and Leo Lenox after the library's founders. They gained the more popular nicknames Patience and Fortitude from Mayor Fiorello La Guardia during the Great Depression. Facing the library, Patience is on your left (south) and Fortitude is to the right (north).

Croton Distributing Reservoir

9. This was once home to the **Croton Distributing Reservoir**, which stored drinking water from the Croton River in Westchester. The foundation of the Reservoir can still be seen in the Library's South Court.

Landmark clock of Sherry's Hotel

10. Head north on Fifth Avenue, toward 44th Street. **Sherry's Hotel** moved here in 1898, to a building designed by McKim, Mead & White; spot it by the landmark clock located outside. The hotel was a symbol of Gilded Age extravagance—once hosting a dinner where guests dined on horseback—until Prohibition shut it down in 1919.

Horseback dinner

11. One block up Fifth Avenue, at 45th Street, you will see the landmark **Fred F. French Building**, named after the founder of Tudor City. Notice its gold embellishments and decorative motifs inspired by the Hanging Gardens of Babylon.

Diamond District

12. As you continue walking north on Fifth Avenue glance down 47th Street. This is known as the **Diamond District**. Over ninety percent of

Rockefeller Center

Radio city Music Hall

Prometheus

St. Patrick's Cathedral

Atlas statue

the diamonds that enter the United States come through New York, and most of those stop here.

13. At 50th Street you will reach **Rockefeller Center** on your left. One of the most beautiful and well-known landmarks in Manhattan, this Art Deco building complex contains **Radio City Music Hall**, the **International Building**, as well as shops and dining in the underground Concourse. The plaza is filled with artwork and ornamentation, including Isamu Noguchi's *News*, a stainless steel bas-relief over the entrance of the **Associated Press Building**.

14. The centerpiece of Rockefeller Center is the **Comcast Building**, the home to NBC Studios. Take a moment to view the lobby at "30 Rock", featuring the mural *American Progress*, painted by Jose Maria Sert. The mural replaced a controversial work by famed Mexican muralist Diego Rivera, deemed unacceptable by Nelson Rockefeller for its depiction of Vladimir Lenin.

15. Exit the Comcast Building and walk along the edge of the sunken plaza. Here you will see Paul Manship's famous gilded sculpture, ***Prometheus***. In the winter the plaza is an ice-skating rink, in summer, an outdoor restaurant.

16. As you continue toward Fifth Avenue, take a moment to relax in the **Channel Gardens**. Named for the English Channel, the gardens separate La Maison Francaise and the British Empire Building. The space frequently hosts public art installations.

17. **St. Patrick's Cathedral** is across the street. The Neo-Gothic structure is an oasis of calm in Midtown, and it's worth a trip inside. Designed by James Renwick, construction began in 1858 and

lasted until 1878. The church is richly decorated, including stained-glass windows from Chartres, France and two altars designed by Tiffany & Co.

647 Fifth Ave (right)

18. From the center aisle, turn and look out the doors—for a direct view of Lee Lawrie's famous *Atlas* statue.

19. Exit the cathedral and turn right, continuing north on Fifth Avenue, past the Versace store (**647 Fifth Avenue**). When the Italian luxury label opened here in 1996, this was the dilapidated former home of George W. Vanderbilt, the grandson of Cornelius Vanderbilt.

647 Fifth Ave, c. 1905

20. Turn left (west) down West 52nd Street. During Prohibition, this was known as "The Street" for its abundant speakeasies and jazz clubs. Today, you can still visit one of the most famous, the **21 Club**—formerly known as Jack and Charlie's 21—at 21 West 52nd Street. Thirty-three jockey statues line its facade.

21 Club

21. Travel east on 52nd Street, across Fifth Avenue. Make a right on Madison Avenue and continue south toward 50th Street. At the northeast corner of 50th Street and Madison Avenue stands the New York Palace Hotel.

West 52nd Street, 1948

22. Here, in 1882, Stanford White built the **Villard Mansion**, six private Italianate residences. When, in the 1970s, they were re-imagined as the Helmsley Palace Hotel, the Landmarks Preservation Committee prohibited demolition of the original structure. So Emery Roth and Sons designed a contemporary fifty-five-story tower above the structure. The hotel opened in 1980, and got a new taste of fame with its starring role on hit series *Gossip Girl*.

Villard Mansion

59th St. and Fourth Ave., 1874

St. Bartholomew's

23. Continue along 50th Street to Park Avenue. Until about 1875 Park Avenue was dirty and undesirable, because of the trains that ran along the then-named Fourth Avenue.

24. On the eastern side of Park Avenue, across 50th Street from the **Waldof-Astoria**, you will approach **St. Bartholomew's Episcopal Church**. Founded in 1835, it moved to this Byzantine-style building in 1918.

25. The bronze doors at St. Bart's were designed by Stanford White in memory of Cornelius Vanderbilt II, the beloved grandson of Cornelius Vanderbilt.

Then and Now
Midtown

Grand Central Terminal, 1903

Longacre (Times) Square, 1904

Fifth Avenue and 51st Street, c. 1900

UPPER WEST SIDE

The area of Manhattan west of Central Park is one of the most densely populated neighborhoods in the entire nation. It's also one of New York City's largest landmark districts, where rows of historic brownstones along tree-lined streets, built circa 1900, are mingled with magnificent apartment houses along Central Park West and the Hudson River.

START:
The Ansonia
2109 Broadway

END:
Strawberry Fields
(Central Park)

TOUR TIME:
About 1.5 hours

CHAPTERS:
13, 18

The Ansonia

Historic brownstones

Columbus Avenue

1. **The Ansonia** is one of the neighborhood's first apartment houses, located on Broadway between 73rd Street and 74th Street. It was built in 1899 as a hotel where guests checked in for months, or even years at a time. For many years its top-floor tenants were Broadway impresario Florenz Ziegfeld and his wife Bille Burke (Glinda in *The Wizard of Oz*), though Ziegfeld kept another apartment for ex-wife Anna Held on the floor below plus a tenth-floor apartment for his paramour Lillian Lorraine! Other residents included Enrico Caruso, Arturo Toscanini, Igor Stravinsky, and opera star Ezio Pinza. Decades later, its ground floor gained even greater notoriety as The Continental Baths, the gay bathhouse that launched the career of Bette Midler.

2. Take a right onto West 74th Street, heading east toward Central Park.

3. While walking on 74th Street, cross Amsterdam Avenue and observe the historic brownstones in this landmark neighborhood. Though many alterations have occurred over the decades (many stoops were removed), these buildings were once erected as single-family dwellings. Today, most have been divided into several apartments.

4. On Columbus Avenue, turn left (north). It's an important shopping street for residents of this neighborhood, with many boutiques and one-of-a-kind restaurants.

5. Continue walking uptown, past the William J. O'Shea Jr. High School. At the corner of 77th Street and Columbus Avenue, turn right.

6. Walk east, on 77th Street toward Central Park.

On the left, you'll pass the **American Museum of Natural History**, famous for its dinosaur skeleton exhibits, also home to the equally astounding Hayden Planetarium.

7. On the right, you'll view some important apartment houses with magnificent views over Central Park. Renowned artist Helen Frankenthaler lived and worked here for years.

8. Continue walking toward Central Park. At the corner (170 Central Park West) is the **New-York Historical Society**, a museum of New York's history, which features a reference library and important archive collection.

9. Cross the street to walk along the sidewalk beside Central Park.

10. This is an ideal vantage point for viewing the magnificent apartment houses that line **Central Park West** in both directions, built before World War II, including several by eminent architect Emery Roth. Almost all are co-ops, where current residents decide to accept or reject potential new neighbors. With that kind of security, these buildings are home to many celebrities. Some residents past and present include: Dustin Hoffman, Katie Couric, Liz Smith, Mary Tyler Moore, Bono, and Madonna; the list goes on and on.

11. Then turn and head downtown (south). The building directly ahead, between 73rd Street and 72nd Street is **The Dakota**. Built in 1884, it was the first building to be erected in this neighborhood, when Central Park was actually an undesirable collection of shanties built by squatters. The Dakota is famous as the first luxury apartment

AMNH on 77th Street

Helen Frankenthaler

AMNH on Central Park West

New-York Historical Society

Central Park West

279

The Dakota

Skating in Central Park, 1890s

Strawberry Fields

house in America. The building has been home to a seemingly endless list of celebrities that has included Boris Karloff, Leonard Bernstein, Lauren Bacall, Rudolf Nureyev, Roberta Flack, Rosemary Clooney, Jason Robards, José Ferrer, and many more. It is also remembered as the sad place where John Lennon was assassinated by Mark David Chapman as he returned home with Yoko Ono from the Record Plant Studio on December 8, 1980.

12. At the corner of 72nd Street, turn left (east) and enter Central Park.

13. Walk straight ahead, bearing to the left, where you'll see a blacktop path and sign labeled **Strawberry Fields**. Follow this path as it curves to the right in the shady park. You'll soon encounter a memorial to the late John Lennon, a place to relax or to explore Central Park.

Then and Now
Central Park

Pond, 1933

Mall, c. 1900

Bow Bridge, before 1901

HARLEM

Harlem is a district that is comprised of several neighborhoods. Here are three areas of historic interest that can be explored separately on foot: Astor Row, Strivers' Row, and Sugar Hill.

W 155th St

Jackie
Robinson
Park

W 150th St

W 147th St

Harlem River Dr

W 145th St

2

1

Sugar Hill

W 142nd St

Convent Ave

St. Nicholas Ave

Edgecombe Ave

Frederick Douglass Blvd

Lenox Ave

The City
College of
New York

4

3 **2** **1**

W 138th St

Strivers' Row

St. Nicholas
Park

W 135th St

Adam Clayton Powell Jr Blvd

Malcolm X Blvd

Fifth Ave

Astor Row

Amsterdam Ave

1

W 130th St

MORNINGSIDE
HEIGHTS

HARLEM

W 128th St

2

tin Luther King Blvd

W 125th St **7** **6** **3** **5**

START:
Fifth Avenue at 130th Street

END:
The Apollo Theater

TOUR TIME:
About 1 hour

CHAPTERS:
21

Astor Row

Sylvia's Restaurant

55 West 125th Street

Astor Row

Much of today's Harlem was purchased as undeveloped land by John Jacob Astor. His grandson William Backhouse Astor developed the rare block of townhouses located between Fifth Avenue and Lenox Avenue on 130th Street, now known as Astor Row, protected as a New York City landmark for their rare wooden porches and front yards.

1. At Fifth Avenue walk west on 130th Street, observing **Astor Row**. At the corner of Lenox Avenue, turn left (south) to walk down Lenox Avenue.

2. You'll pass **Sylvia's Restaurant** (between 126th and 127th streets), a local landmark, serving soul food to Harlem residents and famous visitors since 1962. Every politician visiting Harlem, from Nelson Mandela to Bill Clinton, has dined at Sylvia's Restaurant of Harlem.

3. Continue walking south on Lenox Avenue (also known as Malcolm X Boulevard) to the corner of 125th Street; then turn left (east).

4. Although 125th Street is often called the "Main Street" of Harlem, it's alternate name is actually Martin Luther King, Jr. Boulevard.

5. The offices of President Bill Clinton are located at **55 West 125th Street**, in the middle of the block between Lenox Avenue and Fifth Avenue.

6. Remain on 125th Street by turning around and walking to the west.

7. Cross Lenox Avenue and Seventh Avenue (also known as Adam Clayton Powell, Jr. Boulevard).

Directly ahead at 253 West 125th Street, you'll see the **Apollo Theater**, a National Historic Landmark.

8. Built in 1913, the Apollo Theater has been refurbished several times and is now owned by the State of New York. Originally a burlesque theater, in 1934 the Apollo introduced its famous Amateur Night contests that launched the careers of countless performers. That year, seventeen-year-old Ella Fitzgerald won $25 as an Apollo amateur; her prolific career and an Apollo tradition were born. Some other famous performers (though not amateurs) at the Apollo include: Billie Holiday, Aretha Franklin, James Brown, Stevie Wonder, Marvin Gaye, Luther Vandross, Diana Ross, the Jackson 5, and many more. The lobby and gift shop are open to visitors during business hours.

Apollo Theater

Billie Holiday at Apollo Theater

Strivers' Row

Born in 1865, at the end of the Civil War, Adam Clayton Powell, Sr. was the son of an African-Cherokee slave woman and a white slave owner. It was his stepfather, a former slave, who introduced a young Powell to the Bible. He studied theology at the Yale Divinity School and became pastor of the Abyssinian Baptist Church in Harlem in 1908. As the black population of Harlem grew exponentially, Reverend Powell was its dynamic leader, uniting the community into one of the largest Protestant congregations anywhere in America. He was an early leader in the National Urban League and the NAACP, and a charismatic lecturer.

In 1937, his son Adam Clayton Powell, Jr. succeeded him as pastor of the Abyssinian Baptist Church, after attending nearby City College and Columbia University. The younger Powell used the strength of Harlem's large population to crusade for jobs and housing. He forced the utility

START:
Abyssinian Baptist Church

END:
Striver's Row

TOUR TIME:
About 1 hour

CHAPTERS:
21

The Abyssinian Baptist Church

Strivers' Row

Bill "Bojangles" Robinson

Old horse path

Townhouses by Stanford White

companies to hire black employees, and organized a bus boycott until 200 black workers were hired by the transit authority. Adam Clayton Powell, Jr. was the first black man to be elected to the New York City Council in 1941, and just three years later he was elected to the U.S. House of Representatives as the delegate from Harlem, the first black Congressman from New York.

1. Start at Lenox Avenue (Malcolm X Boulevard) and 138th Street and walk west toward Adam Clayton Powell, Jr. Boulevard. **The Abyssinian Baptist Church** is in the middle of the block. (Everyone is welcome for Sunday services, but the place is always packed, so plan to arrive very early.)

2. Cross 138th Street at the corner of Adam Clayton Powell Jr. Boulevard to visit one of Harlem's most important blocks, known as **Strivers' Row**. In Harlem's heyday, these townhouses were the homes for songwriters Eubie Blake and Noble Sissle, "father of the blues" W. C. Handy, comedian Stepin Fetchit, singer-dancer Bill "Bojangles" Robinson, and Adam Clayton Powell, Jr. Continue walking west along Strivers' Row.

3. At the corner of Frederick Douglass Boulevard, turn right (north). Halfway up the block you will see the entrance to the alley where owners of Strivers' Row townhouses stabled their horses. Today they are garages, a rare commodity anywhere in Manhattan.

4. Continue walking north on Frederick Douglass Boulevard. At the corner of 139th Street, turn right (east) to observe the other side of Strivers' Row. The townhouses on the north side of 139th Street were all designed and decorated by famed architect Stanford White.

Sugar Hill

Sugar Hill is possibly the most beautiful neighborhood in Harlem. While most of the hills and valleys throughout Manhattan were leveled over a century ago, this hill remained intact, with elegant townhouses built on its high ground. Located a few blocks north of **City College of New York (CCNY)**, in an area of Harlem called Hamilton Heights, the Sugar Hill Historic District officially extends from West 145th Street to West 155th Street, bounded by Edgecombe Avenue on the east and Amsterdam Avenue on the west.

The neighborhood got its name in the 1920s when it was a symbol of the "sweet life" available to upscale African-Americans in Harlem. It was declared both a Historic District by the New York City Landmarks Preservation Commission in 2000, and a National Registered Historic Place.

1. **Convent Avenue** is the center boulevard of the landmark district. To view the architecture of this historic place, start at Convent Avenue at West 145th Street.

2. Head north toward West 155th Street, winding your way through the attractive tree-lined streets both to the east and west of Convent Avenue.

3. Famous residents here have included Chief Justice Thurgood Marshall, bandleader Duke Ellington and composer Billy Strayhorn.

4. End your tour at West 155th Street, the neighborhood's northern boundary.

START:
Convent Avenue at 145th Street

END:
Convent Avenue at 155th Street

TOUR TIME:
About 1 hour

CHAPTERS:
21

City College of New York

Convent Avenue

Tree-lined street

TOWNHOUSE STYLE

Labels like Greek Revival, Anglo-Italianate, and Federal, among other terms, define architectural variances in New York's historical real estate. Listed chronologically, these townhouse styles illustrate a brief history of residential construction in New York.

COLONIAL / GEORGIAN
ERA: Prior to the Revolutionary War
DISTINGUISHING TRAITS: wooden exterior, pointed roof
HISTORY: The oldest houses in New York are also its most rare. Fewer than ten wooden houses remain on Manhattan island. Built before the grid was devised for Manhattan's streets, wooden houses were erected on gently rolling farmland. Situated in erratic locations that didn't conform to the visions of city planners, most were demolished. Although the interiors of these last Colonial houses have been drastically renovated to accommodate modern plumbing and storage, their exteriors are landmarks as they are the oldest constructions still standing in urban America.

EARLY FEDERAL
ERA: 1780 to 1810
DISTINGUISHING TRAITS: Exterior red brick walls, usually three stories tall, with pointed roofs to accommodate the run-off from the severe weather the British builders anticipated. Stabilized by an extra-strong brick pattern known as Flemish Bond, each room has a fireplace except on the top floor, where a short chimney risked downdrafts that might blow burning embers onto the wooden floors.
HISTORY: With low ceilings and no ornamentation, these were not popular houses to restore since few New Yorkers would choose to live the spartan life of the city's early residents.
BEST SEEN IN: the landmark district west of Sixth Avenue, below Houston Street (Charlton Street, King Street, Vandam Street). Look for the pointed roofs.

LATE FEDERAL

ERA: 1810 to 1830s

DISTINGUISHING TRAITS: Flat roofs, exterior walls constructed of bricks, with wooden beams set within them, spanning the full width of the house. The house has no "bearing walls" except for the actual brick exterior itself.

HISTORY: Since their architects were schooled in England, Federal houses draw heavily from concepts employed in England, including the "English basement." From the sidewalk, a short stoop leads up to the parlor floor, while a short stair downwards provides the service entrance to the ground-floor kitchen. There is no cellar below. As decades rolled by, it became apparent that New York was not a land of daily rain. Progressing to a flat roof, owners gained desperately needed space on the top floor. To display their newfound prosperity, Federal houses display the first traces of ornamentation, especially around the single front door, with slender pillars, leaded sidelight windows, and lead-glass transoms.

BEST SEEN IN: Greenwich Village, especially west of Bleecker Street; Perry Street, Bank Street, Jane Street and environs. Easily identified by the brick facades.

GREEK REVIVAL

ERA: 1820 to 1840

DISTINGUISHING TRAITS: Similar to a Federal townhouse, built of brick, but with Ionic or Doric columns flanking the single front door, as well as a taller, more imposing stoop. While these houses feature a separate service entrance under the stoop, they also include a full height cellar below grade.

HISTORY: As New York residents prospered, that success was displayed in the heights of their houses and ceilings. The exterior ornamentation provides a hint of the details installed within: elaborate doors of mahogany or rosewood separate the two main parlor rooms, while moldings feature a Greek key or Dentil pattern above. Wainscoting or chair rails wrap around the room, while floors are often planks one-foot wide and one inch thick. Still, city life was far from genteel. Those charming gardens behind today's townhouses had a brutally practical domestic application for the original residents. With the kitchen always situated on the ground floor rear, the yard beyond the kitchen door was the place where pigs were butchered and carpets beaten. Since the city government didn't begin to install plumbing under the streets until the 1830s, it was the site of the cistern and the outhouse.

BEST SEEN IN: Greenwich Village, along the north side of Washington Square, and Chelsea's Cushman Row, 406-418 West 20th Street.

GOTHIC REVIVAL

ERA: 1830s to 1850s

DISTINGUISHING TRAITS: The iconic brownstone arrives. Built of bricks like a Greek Revival townhouse, but faced with a layer of brownstone. Hard Greek symmetry is exchanged for graceful arches.

HISTORY: A romantic movement was sweeping through art and literature. As Henry David Thoreau, the Hudson River School artists, James Fenimore Cooper, and Washington Irving glorified nature, architects responded by applying natural brownstone to the facades, learning to work in a medium that would soon soar in demand. Ornamental features like repeating floral patterns and curves were put to more successful use on Trinity Church (on Broadway at Wall Street, completed in 1846) than in local residences.

BEST SEEN IN: Brooklyn Heights: Willow Street, State Street, Pierrepont Street, and environs. Also visible in some of Manhattan's finest churches, including St. Patrick's Cathedral and Grace Church.

THE BROWNSTONE ERA

By 1850, New York was the most prosperous city in America. Its population tripled over thirty years, driving a nonstop building boom. Houses got smaller but were built more rapidly, with interior decorations ordered from architectural catalogs. "Gingerbread" ornamentation became the order of the day, as self-made aristocrats flaunted their success in pliable brownstone carvings. Some of those styles include:

ITALIANATE
ERA: 1850 to 1880

DISTINGUISHING TRAITS: Rusticated or rough-hewn brownstone at the bottom, smooth brownstone above. Corinthian columns at the double front door, garlands molded into the cornices. Marble mantels in every room.

HISTORY: Monumental in style, patterned after the Italian palazzi, the look suited freestanding mansions like those that once faced Riverside Drive, as well as row houses from Murray Hill to the Upper West Side. With gaslights in the walls of every room, plus two indoor toilets, these brownstones defined the standards of modern convenience.

BEST SEEN: Scattered throughout Manhattan and Brooklyn; these are probably the most plentiful brownstones in New York.

ANGLO-ITALIANATE
ERA: 1850 to 1880

DISTINGUISHING TRAITS: Opulent interior decorations including carved ceilings, carved mantels, and parquet floors appealed to the new merchant class. By applying Italianate style carvings to the exterior brownstone, but repeating it across many buildings in the English fashion, this hybrid was born.

HISTORY: With two rooms on each floor, separated by doors that slide out of view, these highly desirable brownstones provided flexibility for entertaining, and confinement when retaining fireplace heat in winter. These were the first houses to feature closets, with pegs on three sides to hang clothing, as well as dumbwaiters, gas cooking, and hot-air furnaces.

BEST SEEN ON: 16th Street between Second and Third avenues, 70th Street off Central Park West, and West 9th, 10th, and 12th Streets off lower Fifth Avenue (notably Renwick Terrace, 20-38 West 10th Street).

NEO-GREC

ERA: 1870 to 1900

DISTINGUISHING TRAITS: Foregoing the stoop, a new formality is introduced. Guests enter on street level into first-floor reception rooms, often featuring grand staircases. Exteriors use a variety of materials, all culminating in the bold cornices atop each building. When Thomas Edison successfully generated electricity to Manhattan subscribers in 1882, a new modern architecture was born, which soon included elevators, and previously unimaginable kitchen amenities.

HISTORY: Unlike the protruding ornamentation seen on many west-side brownstones, a new understated look of incising into the stone and glass, known as the "Eastlake motif" and "Neo-Grec fluting," is introduced on these elegant townhouses. Built deeply on their lots, with little outdoor space, these dense buildings are costly to maintain, but highly desirable for foundations, private clubs, medical offices, embassies, and consulates.

BEST SEEN ON: East 70s between Fifth and Park avenues; often the most costly townhouses on the market, due to their size, location, and rarity.

QUEEN ANNE

ERA: 1870 to 1900

DISTINGUISHING TRAITS: Breaking the symmetry of earlier construction, rows of Queen Anne style houses are constructed of the same materials, but each exterior varies in design. The result is a visually exciting challenge to the norm.

HISTORY: As America contemplated its Centennial in 1876, an interest in its early architecture re-emerged. Breaking the sleekness of Neo-Grec designs, Queen Anne houses are smaller than most Federal houses, but are notable for the intricate "gingerbread" ornamentation inside and out. While carved garlands may be back on the facade, many Queen Anne houses forego the cornices on top in exchange for pointed or stepped rooflines, each of them different from their neighbors. Ceilings are low, stairs are narrow, but Queen Annes are the jewels of townhouse design.

BEST SEEN ON: East 80s, near York Avenue.

Eventually, New Yorkers tired of the monumental streetscapes and showy ornamentation of row houses. They tired of the stairs, the sooty fireplaces, and the limited storage space.

Blame it on The Dakota: When America's first luxury apartment house opened in 1884, the real estate market went spinning in an exciting new direction. Filled with as much ornamentation as a block of Queen Anne townhouses, The Dakota offered spacious homes without stairs, luxurious bathrooms, and something that townhouse owners never considered: views. While townhouses were constructed sporadically over the ensuing years, the arrival of luxury apartments slowed new townhouse construction. Rows of them were razed to make room for new high-rise construction, as more people squeezed into New York's five boroughs. Freestanding mansions toppled too, as developers met the demand for luxury apartment construction.

Today, the finite number of townhouses remaining in New York comprises some of its most valuable real estate. With more than half of Manhattan's townhouses protected by landmark status, they're also a romantic reminder of the city's history.

View of lower Manhattan from Brooklyn He...

INDEX

BIBLIOGRAPHY

Anbinder, Tyler, *Five Points*, The Free Press, New York, 2001.

Baker, Paul R., *Stanny: The Gilded Life of Stanford White*, The Free Press, a division of MacMillan Inc., New York, 1989.

Batterberry, Michael and Ariane, *On The Town In New York*, Scribner, New York, 1973.

Beard, Rick, and Berlowitz, Leslie Cohen, editors, *Greenwich Village: Culture and Counterculture*, published for the Museum of the City of New York by Rutgers University Press, New Brunswick, New Jersey, 1993.

Birmingham, Stephen, *Life At The Dakota*, Random House, NY 1979.

Bookbinder, Bernie, *City of the World: New York and its People*, Harry N. Abrams, Inc. New York, 1989.

Brown, Henry Collins, *Fifth Avenue Old and New*, official publication of the Fifth Avenue Association, Wynkoop Hallenbeck Crawford Co., New York, 1924.

Casill, Peter, *New York Memories of Yesteryear*, Exposition Press, New York, 1964.

Caro, Robert A., *The Power Broker*, Knopf, New York, 1989.

Daley, Robert, *The World Beneath the City*, J.B. Lippincott Company, Philadelphia and New York, 1959.

Delaney, Edmund T., *New York's Turtle Bay - Old and New*, Barre Publishers, Barre, Massachusetts, 1965.

Dunlop, M. H., *Gilded City*, HarperCollins Publishers, Inc. New York, 2000.

Ellis, Edward Robb, *The Epic of New York City*, Coward McCann Inc., New York, 1966.

Federal Writers Project, *New York City Guide*, Random House, New York, 1939.

Federal Writers Project, *New York Panorama*, Random House, New York, 1938.

Foreman, John, and Pierce Stimson, Robbe. *The Vanderbilts and the Gilded Age, New York*: St. Martins Press, 1991.

Garmey, Stephen, *Gramercy Park: An Illustrated History of a New York Neighborhood*, Balsam Press Inc., Rutledge Books, New York, 1984.

Gayle, Margot, and Gillon, Edmund V., *Cast-Iron Architecture in New York*, Dover Publications, Inc., New York, 1974.

Gaylord, R. Bruce Cranor, *The Picture Book of Greenwich Village*, Carol Publishing Group, New York 1991.

George-Warren, Holly, editor: *The Roll-ing Stone Book of the Beats*, Rolling Stone Press, New York, 1999.

Goldstone, Harmon H., *History Preserved: A Guide to New York City Landmarks*, Simon and Schuster, New York, 1974.

Greenberg, Cheryl Lynn, *"Or Does It Explode?" Black Harlem In The Great Depression*, Oxford University Press, New York, 1997.

Gurock, Jeffrey S., *When Harlem Was Jewish*, Columbia University Press, New York 1979.

Hanley, Rev. Denis J., *A Pictorial History of Early Chinatown*, ARTS Inc., New York, 1980.

Henderson, Mary C., *The City and the Theatre*, James T. White & Company, Clifton, New Jersey, 1973.

Henderson, Mary C., *The New Amsterdam*, Roundtable Press-Hyperion, New York, 1997.

Hindus, Milton, *The Old East Side, an Anthology*, The Jewish Publication Society of America, Philadelphia, PA, 1969.

Homberger, Eric, *The Historical Atlas of New York City*, Henry Holt and Company, New York, 1994.

Jackson, Kenneth T., et.al. *The Encyclopedia of New York City*, New York Historical Society, Yale University Press, New Haven, 1995.

Jackson, Kenneth T., and Dunbar, David S., *Empire City: New York Through the Centuries*, Columbia University Press, New York, 2002.

Jacob Riis. (n.d.). Retrieved October 28, 2009, from http://en.wikipedia.org/wiki/Jacob_Riis

Janvier, Thomas A., *In Old New York*, Harper & Brothers, New York, 1894. Reprinted by St. Martin's Press, New York, April 2000.

King, Robert B. *The Vanderbilt Homes*, New York: Rizzoli International Publications, 1989.

Kahn, Steve, *SoHo New York*, Rizzoli International Publications Inc., New York, 1999.

Lanier, Henry Wysham, *Greenwich Village, Today and Yesterday*, Harper and Brothers, New York, 1949.

Lockwood, Charles, *Bricks and Brownstone*, Abbeville Press, New York, 1972.

Lockwood, Charles, *Manhattan Moves Uptown*, Houghton Mifflin Company, Boston, Massachusetts, 1976.

Lowe, David, *Stanford White's New York*, Doubleday, NY 1992.

Lyman, Susan Elizabeth, *The Story of New York*, Crown Publishers, New York, 1964.

McNamara, Brooks, *The New York Concert Saloon*, Cambridge University Press, Cambridge, UK, 2002.

Miller, Terry, *Greenwich Village And How It Got That Way*, Crown Publishers Inc. New York, 1990.

Mitgang, Herbert, *Once Upon A Time In New York*, The Free Press, a division of Simon & Schuster, New York, 2000.

Moorhouse, Geoffrey, *Imperial City: New York*, Henry Holt and Company, New York 1988.

Mordden, Ethan, *All That Glittered*, St. Martin's Press, New York, 2007.

Patterson, Jerry E., *Fifth Avenue: The Best Address*, Rizzoli International Publications, Inc., New York, 1998.

Perlman, Bennard B., *Painters of the Ashcan School*, Dover Publications Inc., New York 1979.

Plumb, Stephen, *The Streets Where They Lived*, MarLor Press, St. Paul, MN, 1989.

Roskolenko, Harry, *The Time That Was Then*, The Dial Press, New York, 1971.

Rosenzweig, Roy and Blackmar, Elizabeth, *The Park and the People*, Cornell University Press, Ithaca, New York, 1992.

Ruttenbaum, Steven, *Mansions in the Clouds: the Skyscraper Palazzi of Emery Roth*, Balsam Press, New York 1986.

Salwen, Peter, *Upper West Side Story*, Abbeville Press, NY 1989.

Shaw, Arnold, *The Street That Never Slept*, Coward, McCann & Geoghan, Inc. New York, 1971.

Silverberg, Robert, *Light For The World*, D. Van Nostrand Company Inc., New York, 1967.

Tauranac, John, *Essential New York*, Holt Rinehold & Winston, NY 1980.

Trager, James, *Park Avenue: Street of Dreams*, Atheneum, NY 1990.

Trager, James, *West of Fifth: The Rise and Fall and Rise of Manhattan's West Side*, Atheneum, NY 1987.

Willensky, Eliot and White, Norval, *American Institute of Architects Guide to New York City*, third edition, Harcourt Brace Jovanovich, New York, 1988.

Wolfe, Gerard, *New York: A Guide To The Metropolis*, NY University Press, NY, 1978.

Wurman, Richard Saul, *Access: New York City*, HarperCollins, New York, 1997

Interviews: Richard Winkler, Broadway producer, New York, August 17 and August 20, 2015.

ACKNOWLEDGEMENTS

Museyon Guides would like to thank the following individuals and organizations for their guidance and assistance in creating Chronicles of Old New York.

Lower East Side Tenement Museum

Museum of the City of New York

National Park Service, Frederick Law Olmsted National Historic Site

New-York Historical Society

New York Public Library

New York University Archives

Prints & Photographs Division, Library of Congress

Public Theater

Smithsonian Institution, National Portrait Gallery

Susan S. Szenasy, Metropolis Magazine

Brey Brownlie, New York Living Magazine

Karolina Pierz, New York Living Magazine

Ann Simkins, New York Living Magazine

Taka Hayashi, Pepperland

whiskers, ca. 1844-1860, Library of Congress, LC-USZC4-4160

Page 94: The sunken track of the N.Y. and Harlem Railroad, 4th Avenue, above 126 Street, New York City, 1876, Picture Collection, The New York Public Library, Astor, Lenox and Tilden Foundations

Page 97: Vanderbilt Ball, Mrs. Cornelius Vanderbilt as electric light, March 26, 1883, photo by Mora; Costume Ball Photograph Collection, PR-223, Series V, Folder 34; negative no. 39500, Collection of the New-York Historical Society

Page 99: Houses and mansions - Vanderbilt Mansion. Wedding day of Gladys Vanderbilt and Count Laszlo Szechenyi, Jan. 28, 1908, 1908, Library of Congress, LC-USZ62-69597

Page 100: Mayor Gaynor, Col. Roosevelt and Cornelius Vanderbilt on 5th Ave, 1910, Library of Congress, LC-USZ62-60851

Page 105: Wyand, D.E. The Squatters of New York—scene near Central Park, 1869, Library of Congress, LC-USZ62-106378

Page 108: Olmsted Family Photographs, Olmsted Job #1 Frederick Law Olmsted Sr. cap & cape c. 1860, Courtesy of the Nation Park Service, Frederick Law Olmsted National Historic Site

Page 109: Grand Drive, Central Park N.Y., 1869, Published by Currier & Ives, Museum of the City of New York, The Harry T. Peters Collection

Page 113: New York City—serenade given to ex-governor Tilden at his Gramercy Park residence on October 27th 1877, Picture Collection, The New York Public Library, Astor, Lenox and Tilden Foundations

Page 115: Abbott, Berenice. Gramercy Park North #60, Milstein Division of United States History, Local History & Genealogy, The New York Public Library, Astor, Lenox and Tilden Foundations

Page 117: Page 167: Cab stand at Madison Square, 1900, Library of Congress, LC-D401-13619

Flatiron Building, New York, N.Y., 1902, Library of Congress, LC-D401-14278

Clam seller in Mulberry Bend, N.Y., 1900, Library of Congress, LC-D401-13642

Newsboys and newsgirl. (Mary Malchade) (9 years old.) Getting afternoon papers, Park Row, 1910, Library of Congress, LC-USZ62-120557

On the streets in a New York blizzard, 1899, Library of Congress, LC-D4-13621

Hine, Lewis Wickes. Tending Stand, Canal St. Location, 1910, Library of Congress, LC-USZ6-1242

Hine, Lewis Wickes. A load of kimonos just finished. Girl very reticent. Thompson St., 1912, Library of Congress, LC-DIG-nclc-05490

Miss Twombly, whip of Ladies Coach

Run, and two other ladies beside coach on street, New York, Library of Congress, LC-DIG-ggbain-03305

Page 119: New York circa 1905. "Broadway and Times Building (1 Times Square).", Detroit Publishing Company, Library of Congress

Page 129: Käsebier, Gertrude. Evelyn Nesbit about 1900 at a time when she was brought to the studio by Stanford White, 1900, Library of Congress, LC-DIG-ppmsca-12056

Page 131: Madison Square Garden, New York, Library of Congress, LC-D4-12672

Page 134: Mrs. Thos. Hastings's coach leaves Colony Club. 5/10/11. Mrs. A. Iselin, whip, Mrs. Hastings beside her, Mrs. W.G. Loew between, Library of Congress, LC-B2-2230-17

Zane, Steven. Villard Houses, 451-457 Madison Avenue & 24 East Fifty-first Street, New York

Penn Station, New York City, 1920, Library of Congress, LC-USZ62-74598

Page 137: Draper, John William. Dorothy Draper, 1840, New York University Archives, Photographic Collection

Page 140: De Meyer, Adolf, Baron. Three-quarter length portrait of Gertrude Vanderbilt Whitney (Mrs. Harry Payne Whitney) wearing a jeweled gown and tiara and holding a peacock feather fan, 1916, Library of Congress, LC-USZC2-6127

Orchard Street on a Sunday morning, 1915

Page 145: Manhattan: Central Park West, west side btw. 72nd Street and 73rd Street, Milstein Division of United States History, Local History & Genealogy, The New York Public Library, Astor, Lenox and Tilden Foundations

Page 151: Collins, Marjory. New York, New York. Central Park common on Sunday, Library of Congress, LC-USW3-007791-E

Page 157:New York City circa 1900. "Jewish market on the East Side.", Library of Congress, LC-USZ62-72444

Page 158:Hine, Lewis Wickes. 1 P.M. Family of Onofrio Cottone, 7 Extra Pl., N.Y., finishing garments in a terribly run down tenement. The father works on the street. The three oldest children help the mother on garments. Joseph, 14, Andrew, 10, Rosie, 7, and all together they make about $2 a week when work is plenty. There are two babies. 1913, Library of Congress, LC-DIG-nclc-04305

Page 159: New York · East Side eviction, 1910, Library of Congress, LC-USZ62-30768

Page 161: Niwa, Keiko. Lower East Side Tenement Museum, Courtesy Lower East Side Tenement Museum

Page 163: New York City Deputy Police Commissioner John A. Leach, right, watching agents pour liquor into sewer following a raid during the height of prohibition, 1921, Library of Congress, LC-USZ62-123257

Page 171: Crowd outside the Savoy in Harlem, © Bettmann/CORBIS

Page 172: N.Y.C. street scenes—million dollar corner, 34th St. & Broadway. Small plot which sold for a million dollars, 1911, Library of Congress, LC-USZ62-93589

Page 179: Abbott, Berenice. Triborough Bridge, East 125th Street approach, Manhattan, 1937, Photography Collection, Miriam and Ira D. Wallach Division of Art, Prints and Photographs, The New York Public Library, Astor, Lenox and Tilden Foundations

Page 181: Spieglitz, C.M. Sponsor of Battery Bridge/ World Telegram & Sun, Library of Congress, LC-USZ62-136079

Page 187: Ginsberg, Allen. William S. Burroughs, Lucien Carr and Allen Ginsberg, 1953, © Allen Ginsberg/ CORBIS

Page 189: Vachon, John. New York, New York. Times Square on a rainy day, 1943, Library of Congress, LC-USW3-020251-E

Page 190: Actor Montgomery Clift, far left, and Jack Kerouac, far right (along with several other unidentified diners), eat at the San Remo Cafe. San Remo Collection, Greenwich Village Society for Historic Preservation

Page 195: Broadway, North from Spring Street, 1898, Museum of the City of New York, Byron Collection, Gift of Percy Byron, 1942

Page 197: Rau, William H. Busy Broadway, north from Prince Street, New York City, 1904, Library of Congress, LC-USZ62-94237

Page 198: The first cast-iron house erected at New York, from The Illustrated London News, 1851, Pictures Collection, The New York Public Library, Astor, Lenox and Tilden Foundations

Page 205: General Theological Seminary, [Chelsea, New York], 1900, Library of Congress, LC-DIG-det-4a20060

Page206: Clement C. Moore by Matthew Brady Studio, National Portrait Gallery, Smithsonian Institution, Frederick Hill Meserve Collection, Meserve.1127:40

Page 209: Gottscho, Samuel H. New York City views. Rockefeller Center and RCA Building from 515 Madison Ave., 1933, Library of Congress, LC-G612-T01-21012-Ax

Page 212: Firemen searching for bodies, 1911, Library of Congress, LC-USZ62-83864

Page 213: Harris & Ewing. U.S. Ambassador to Great Britain. Washington, D.C., Dec. 9, 1939, Library of Congress, LC-H22-D-7951

Page 214: John D. Rockefeller, full-length portrait, walking on street with John D. Rockefeller, Jr., 1915, Library of Congress, LC-USZ62-48511

Page 220: City Hall, New York, Library of Congress, LC-D4-17237

Page 230: Mulberry Street, New York City, 1900, Library of Congress, LC-D401-12683

Page 238: Abbott, Berenice. Milk wagon and old houses, Grove Street, No. 4-10, Manhattan, 1936, Photography Collection, Miriam and Ira D. Wallach Division of Art, Prints and Photographs, The New York Public Library, Astor, Lenox and Tilden Foundations

Page 246: Hine, Lewis Wickers. The breaking point. A heavy load for an old woman. Lafayette St., below Astor Pl., N.Y., 1912, Library of Congress, LC-DIG-nclc-04165

Page 211: Dick, Archibald L. after, James H. Darkin. La Grange Terrace, La Fayette Place, City of New York. [1831-1834], I.N. Phelps Stokes Collection, Miriam and Ira D. Wallach Division of Art, Prints and Photographs, The New York Public Library, Astor, Lenox and Tilden Foundations

Page 213: Gottscho, Samuel, H. New York city views. Night view of plaza buildings, over park lake, night, 1933, Library of Congress, LC-G612-T01-19557

Vachon, John. New York, New York. Camel cigarette advertisement at Times Square, 1943, Library of Congress, LC-USW3-018258-D

Mott Street, New York, N.Y., 1905, Library of Congress, LC-D4-18616

Page 254: Abbott, Berenice. Gramercy Park, nos. 3-5, Manhattan, 1935, Photography Collection, Miriam and Ira D. Wallach Division of Art, Prints and Photographs, The New York Public Library, Astor, Lenox and Tilden Foundations

Page 260: Gottscho, Samuel H. River House, 52nd St. and E. River, New York City. Cloud study, noon, looking south from 27th floor, Library of Congress, LC-G612-T01-17489

Page 276: The Dakota (Apartments), 1 West Seventy-second Street, Central Park West, New York, New York County, NY, Library of Congress, HABS NY,31-NEYO, 74-

Page 282: Untitled [Harlem street scene], 1944, Museum of the City of New York, Gift of the Department of Local Government, Public Record Office of South Australia

Page 304: Sunday morning at Orchard and Rivington, New York City, 1915, Library of Congress, LC-USZ62-72444

ABOUT MUSEYON

Named after the Museion, the ancient Egyptian institute dedicated to the muses, Museyon Guides is an independent publisher that explores the world through the lens of cultural obsessions. Intended for frequent fliers and armchair travelers alike, our books are expert-curated and carefully researched, offering rich visuals, practical tips and quality information.

MUSEYON ADULT TITLES

Pick one up and follow your interests...wherever they might go.
For more information vist **www.museyon.com**. www.facebook.com/museyon and www. twitter.com/museyon. Inquiries: info@museyon.com

MUSEYON INC.
Publisher: Akira Chiba
Editor: Heather Corcoran
Editor: Janice Battiste

Assistant Editor: Mackenzie Allison
Cover Design: José Antonio Contreras

Museyon Guides has made every effort to verify that all information included in this guide is accurate and current as of our press date. All details are subject to change.

ACCLAIMED CHRONICLES SERIES

"Evokes a strong sense of place"
    –New York Times

"Lovely, gorgeous and intelligent"
    –Chicago Tribune

"Packs a good bit of history into one handy source"
    –Publishers Weekly

"Graphics that pop, plenty of maps and a breezy tone"
    –Los Angeles Times

"This little gem is as much fun for the armchair traveler
as it is for the tourist"   *–Library Journal*

ABOUT THE AUTHOR

A third-generation New Yorker, James Roman has regaled listeners with his chronicles of old New York as a real estate broker and sales manager for fifteen years in Manhattan, and as a lecturer at the Real Estate Board of New York and New York University. He served as Editorial Contributor to *New York Living* magazine for six years, and contributes regularly to publications that document emerging technology. Readers can find him on re-runs of the HBO television series *Six Feet Under*, a break he attributes more to luck than to acumen.